AudioCraft

**An Introduction
To The Tools
And Techniques
Of Audio
Production**

Second Edition

RANDY THOM

NATIONAL FEDERATION OF COMMUNITY BROADCASTERS

ACKNOWLEDGMENTS

The first edition of *AudioCraft* was primarily the work of Randy Thom. Many others contributed their time and talents to produce that volume, including Theresa R. Clifford, Chris Merrick, Betsy Rubinstein, Jake Schumacher, David R. Taylor, and Thomas J. Thomas.

This second edition built upon that work. Randy Thom updated the book. Kim Aubrey provided technical review; Lynn Chadwick revived the effort and edited it; Sandra R. Walker assisted with production; and David LePage provided the financial and market planning. Our combined efforts made this second edition possible.

Funding from the National Endowment for the Arts provided the initial support that made the idea of a second edition a reality.

Illustration

Ed Anzilotti, *pages 28, 34, 49, 53, 54, 69, 70, 71, 83, 104*

Gail Chase, *pages 12, 13, 42, 55, 65, 81, 82, 92, 124, 128, 153*

Tim Flatt, *page 129*

J. Michael, *pages 59, 62, 115, 116, 117*

Randy Thom, *page 20*

Andrea Z. Tachiera, *pages 6, 7, 47*

Photography

AKG Acoustics, *page 36*

Ampex, *pages 42, 44, 50, 51, 52, 54*

Joseph Greco, *pages 32, 35, 37, 57, 58, 61, 66, 77, 98, 103, 114*

Lexicon, *page 107*

Sound Workshop Professional Audio Products, *page 68*

Tom Thomas, *page 118*

Karla Tonella, *pages 33, 45, 49, 56, 94, 98*

Design by Page Designs Unlimited

Contents

PREFACE

AudioCraft: An Introduction to the Tools and Techniques of Audio Production has been widely recognized by professionals at radio stations and universities as a single, comprehensive text that guides the novice producer from early concepts to finished work. It is designed both for organized courses and for self-teaching. It is written so that it can be understood by those without science and engineering backgrounds, and will be useful to performers, announcers, producers and others who use the medium of sound. While *AudioCraft* is written primarily with radio production in mind, it will also benefit people working in video, film, and audio/visual presentations.

This second edition of *AudioCraft* is updated with information about new audio technologies that continue to evolve even as we write about them.

AudioCraft has been developed from the experience of America's community radio stations. Located in all kinds of communities, from rural areas to major cities, and controlled by organizations of men and women reflecting diverse backgrounds, these stations share a commitment to extensive public participation in both governance and programming.

The unique and important contribution of community radio has been to open the airwaves to thousands of people who are (or were) not radio producers by profession. The cultural and political life of dozens of communities is richer today because these stations have provided the means through which citizens can speak to one another and share their concerns, their convictions and their creativity.

In the Information Age, the electronic media will continue to grow in importance in our national life. We hope that *AudioCraft* will be one resource to enable a far broader range of people—whether as full-time professionals or as skilled volunteers—to use these powerful tools.

Lynn Chadwick
President, National Federation of Community Broadcasters
April, 1989

SOME BASIC THEORY

Before jumping right into turning on the tape recorders, it is useful to consider what is the nature of the work we are about to undertake. A clear understanding of how we use sound in our lives everyday will help when we are trying to produce a meaningful recording in the studio.

In Part One, we discuss basic concepts that will inform every recording activity discussed in later chapters. Mastering these ideas early in your study of audio production will simplify your work later on.

CHAPTER ONE

LISTENING

If you are a newcomer to the "arts" or more particularly to the "media" you may not be aware that there is an ancient rivalry between things visual and things aural. Actually the rivalry may exist more in the minds of the artists who represent two "sides" than it does in the perceptual apparatus of the audience.

Even in film, where the two disciplines can work together powerfully, there is nearly constant friction between the two camps, the sound workers and the picture workers.

It is an enjoyable dispute among professionals. As students of sound, it is important to understand the glories of the ear, and to see (excuse the visual metaphor) a few of the shortcomings of the eyeball crowd.

- There is no time when, if we listen, we won't hear some sound. (The "natural" sounds within any given environment are called *ambience*.)

- Most of us are so accustomed to our eyes and ears working together that we don't often think about them as separate and very different senses. For example, when inexperienced radio reporters are sent to record a press conference, they often stand at the back of the room and hold their microphones in the air in order to pick up the voices of the people speaking in front.

  What these reporters don't realize is that what they see unavoidably augments what they hear, and that their radio audience will not have the advantages of sight. The sight of the speaker's lip movements, facial expressions and body movements all add meaning and intelligibility to the words being spoken. The ability to locate the speaker in a particular part of the room also helps the reporter to ignore sounds coming from other parts of the room.

- The radio listener doesn't receive these clues, and this makes the clarity of the voice recording essential. The closer the microphone is to the person speaking, the easier it will be for the listener to clearly hear what is being said.

- Taking a picture and recording a sound are very different kinds of operations, partly because of the difference in the way light and sound are reflected. Making a good picture is in many ways much easier than making a good recording of a sound, because a visual image is not reflected by its surroundings nearly so much, or so coherently, as is a sound.

  Trying to make a clear recording of somebody speaking indoors is a little like trying to get a single image photograph of somebody who is standing in a room full of mirrors. The only way to get the shot is to move the camera very close to the person, or use a long lens. Likewise, it's usually necessary to place a microphone within a couple of feet of the desired sound source to obtain a clear recording, with a minimum of ambient noise and reverberation.

On the other hand, as a microphone is moved farther away from a sound source more of the "character" of the *acoustic space* will be heard. The environmental sounds that surround our principal sound source, and the echo and reverberation of all those sounds in the acoustic field, may add drama and a sense of realism to what might otherwise be a clear but characterless presentation.

So our radio reporter would be best advised to try two kinds of coverage: (1) close-up recordings of the principal voices and sounds and (2) more distant, environmental coverage that will depict the character of the event as a whole.

- Many artists in a variety of fields, visual as well as aural, have said that music is the most powerfully emotive of all the arts. Remember that any sound placed in an appropriate context can be musical in the most basic sense, and inherit that magical power.

- The silences between words and between notes of music are as valuable in conveying meaning as the sounds themselves; each is meaningless without the other.

- The enormous contribution that sound can make to nearly any media presentation is truly amazing. It can set or augment an emotional tone; define a physical space; distinguish one locale from another; clarify elements of a story, or make them more ambiguous; establish pace; foreshadow action, or recall it; symbolize other story elements; heighten realism, or diminish it; connect otherwise unconnected ideas, etc. Even "silent films" were very rarely silent. They nearly always had musical accompaniment of some kind.

- Sounds, like smells, can often revitalize memories and excite the imagination in ways that visual images may only envy.

KEY TERMS TO REMEMBER

ambience   acoustic space

SOUND

The basic attributes of a sound, by which it is described or compared with another sound, are: its *frequency* (pitch), its *duration* (length of time), its *volume* (loudness) and its *timbre* (tone color—the relative strength of all the component frequencies in a sound). Further, all natural sounds vary in loudness over time—this is called *dynamics*. The range of volumes of any natural sound, from softest to loudest, is referred to as its *dynamic range*.

For example, imagine a conversation involving several people. Some of the people have louder voices than others (volume). Every voice has a basic pitch (bass, treble, or somewhere in between), but each person's voice sounds unique, due, among other things, to the combinations of various frequencies within a voice (timbre).

The conversation lasts for a certain period, as does each word and sentence (duration), and it varies in volume as it progresses (dynamic range). We'll see that each of these characteristics presents specific problems and possibilities.

As sound technicians, we have to consider more than just the source of sound. All sounds happen in an environment. There are likely to be several sources of sound in a given environment—some that we want to record, and some that we don't. Also, all of the surfaces in the environment will affect the way we perceive those sounds. If you and I are having a conversation in a room, much of what we hear of each other's voice will have bounced off the walls, ceiling and floor, rather than having come directly from mouth to ear.

How about the equipment we use to record and process sounds? We can evaluate any piece of audio equipment in three basic ways:

- *Frequency Response*—How well does this device respond to and reproduce all of the frequencies of sound fed into it?

- *Signal-to-Noise Ratio*—How much noise will this device add to the signal (sound) being fed into it?

- *Distortion*—How accurately will this device reproduce the signal that is being fed into it without creating new signals that are related to the original. (For example, when you turn up the volume of your stereo system so loud that you hear crackling sounds superimposed over the music, you are causing the system to "distort.") At least some of the crackling sounds are "harmonics," multiples of the frequencies of the original sounds.

We will present ways to recognize and deal with problems in each of these areas.

FREQUENCY AND HOW IT IS MEASURED

All sounds are caused by something vibrating. The rate of the fundamental vibration determines the pitch (frequency) of the sound—the faster the vibration, the higher the pitch. A guitar string, for instance, that vibrates back and forth two hundred times a second makes a sound that is said to have a frequency of two hundred *cycles per second*. Often, instead of "cycle per second," the word *Hertz* (or "Hz") is used, after a German physicist who made important discoveries about the nature of sound. (Since the metric system is used in science, we refer to a thousand cycles as *kiloHertz*, or "kHz.")

Any single-frequency sound is called a *tone*. "Pure" tones do not occur naturally, and can only be generated artificially. All *natural* sounds are *complex*, i.e., they contain *many* frequencies of sound that are heard simultaneously. The relative strength of the various frequencies composing a sound determine the timbre (tone color) of that sound. That is why, among other reasons, a piano, a baritone sax, a singer, and wind blowing through telephone lines can all produce the "same" note but still sound different.

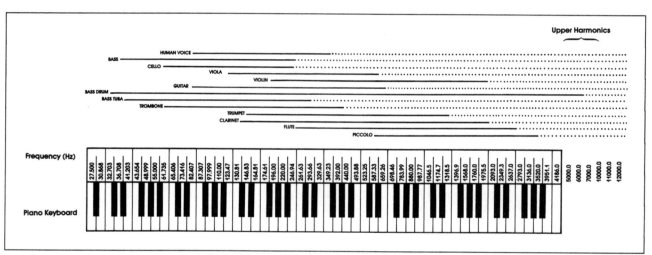

FREQUENCY CHART

Represented here are the parts of the audible spectrum of frequencies occupied by some common musical instruments and the human voice. Though we chose to make 12,000 Hertz our upper limit, most of these sound sources generate frequencies even higher.

The range of frequencies people can hear is approximately from 15 Hz to 20,000 Hz (referred to as the *audio range or spectrum*). Very few people are able to consciously differentiate frequencies at the very top and bottom of this spectrum, but most with good hearing will notice if those frequencies are suddenly removed. The spectrum is commonly subdivided into *low* (bass), *midrange* (mids), and *high* (treble) frequencies:

- LOW = any frequency below approximately 300 Hz
- MIDRANGE = approximately 300 Hz to 3,500 Hz
- HIGH = any frequency above approximately 3,500 Hz

The frequency response of the ear varies from person to person and is affected, among many other things, by age, the amount of prolonged exposure

dB-SPL	
220	12 ft. in front of cannon below muzzle
200	
180	rocket engines
160	jet engine, close up
150	permanent damage to hearing
140	airport runway
130	
120	threshold of pain thunder
110	loud power tools
100	subway
90	heavy truck traffic
80	
70	busy street
60	small party
50	busy office
40	quiet conversation
30	empty office
20	empty living room
10	
0	threshold of hearing

SPL CHART

SPL stands for Sound Pressure Level. The purpose of this chart is to give you some idea of the volumes of several common sounds compared to each other and the threshold of hearing. Obviously each of these examples of sound sources and environments will vary a great deal over time, but the figures quoted here are averages. The word "empty" means unoccupied by people. So, the empty office, for example, will still have sound sources like the hum of printers and ventilation systems.

to very loud sounds, the physical health of the ear, and the amount of wax present.

The highest frequencies are usually the first to go in hearing loss. NOT COINCIDENTALLY, they are also the hardest frequencies for audio equipment to record and reproduce. By the age of twenty, many people can no longer hear frequencies above 15 kHz, and 10 kHz is not an unusual upper limit. This is one of the reasons why tastes vary as to the amount of high frequency signal desirable in music. People who are in the habit of turning up the treble (higher frequencies) when listening to recordings or broadcasts may be doing this to compensate for lack of high frequency response in their ears, of which they may be unaware.

THE DECIBEL —COMPARING THE LOUDNESS OF SOUNDS AND THE LEVELS OF SIGNALS

If we are making a recording of a piece of music, and I notice that the piano, for example, isn't being recorded as loudly as it should be in relation to the other instruments, I need a way to tell you (as the person operating the controls) exactly how much louder I think it should be. If I say, "I think it should be a little louder," your idea of what "little" means may be significantly different from mine. If we are calibrating the tape recorder, accuracy will be even more important. This need to be precise when comparing volumes of different sounds and levels of signals is soon apparent to all of us who work with the medium.

Human ears can hear a wide range of volumes of sound. The loudest sounds we can hear without pain are about 100,000,000,000 times as powerful as the softest sounds we are able to detect.

Working with such large numbers in comparing volumes is awkward, so a logarithmic system of comparison using smaller numbers was devised. The basic unit of this system of comparison is the *decibel* (abbreviated "dB"). We compare different levels by saying that one sound is so many dB more or less than some other sound. A difference of one dB is so slight as to be barely audible. But because the scale is logarithmic, a difference of six dB is substantial, and a difference of twenty dB is very large. A sound that will cause pain to the ear is about 120 decibels louder than a sound that is barely audible, though the exact figure depends on lots of factors, including the frequency of the sound and the sensitivity to sound of the person who is listening.

When we see the term decibel being used in an apparently "absolute" way, as in "The noise in the stadium reached 100 dB." it actually means that the sound level is 100 dB louder than an established reference level (in this case, probably 100dB louder than the threshold of hearing). In other words, the term "dB" cannot be properly used as an absolute, but rather only as a comparative term.

KEY TERMS TO REMEMBER

audio range

complex sound

cycles per second

decibel (dB)

distortion

duration

dynamic range

dynamics

frequency

frequency response

Hertz (Hz)

kiloHertz (kHz)

signal-to-noise ratio

timbre

tone

tone color

volume

CHAPTER THREE

SOUND AND ELECTRICITY—AUDIO

In order to send sounds through wires, amplify them, store them on tape, disk, or broadcast them, they must be converted into electricity. The electrical, magnetic, or optical representation of a sound is called a "signal." To understand this conversion, let's examine one of the most common devices which perform this function: the *microphone*.

All microphones are electrical generators, which produce very tiny amounts of electricity. They change mechanical energy (sound) into electrical energy. There are several ways to do this. Perhaps the design which is easiest to understand is the one used by the so-called "dynamic" microphone.

The *dynamic microphone* contains a magnet and a *diaphragm*, a thin disc which vibrates back and forth as sound waves strike its surface and which in turn vibrates a tiny coil of wire which is an electrical *conductor* (i.e., electrical impulses will flow through it). The magnet, like all magnets, is surrounded by a magnetic field. (The patterns that iron filings form around a magnet illustrate the lines of force which make up a magnet's field.)

Any time an electrical conductor is moved through a magnetic field, an electric current is generated in the conductor.

The diaphragm in a microphone vibrates at the same rate (frequency) and with the same relative *intensity (volume)* as the sound waves which strike it. The rate and intensity of the electrical impulses generated by the movement of the diaphragm are equivalent to the frequency and loudness of the sound which caused the diaphragm to vibrate.

Since the coil is an electrical conductor, its vibration (back and forth movement) in the magnetic field causes a current to flow. Again, the rate (number of vibrations per second) determines the frequency of the electrical signal. The intensity determines the "voltage" or volume. And because the diaphragm moves alternately back and forth, the electrical current which it generates likewise changes in direction, and for that reason is called *alternating current*, or "AC." Thus, the microphone has created an *electrical analog* of an *acoustic* event.

The *intensity* of an electrical current is referred to as its *amplitude*, or *voltage*. As we have seen, the voltage of an electrical current is analogous to the amplitude (volume) of a sound wave.

SOUND	ELECTRICITY
Volume = Intensity = Loudness	**Amplitude = Intensity = Voltage**

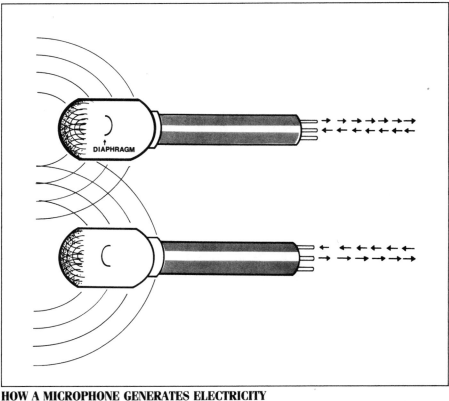

HOW A MICROPHONE GENERATES ELECTRICITY

Here we see the diaphragm in a mic being vibrated back and forth by a sound. As it bends in one direction, it causes an electrical current to flow in one direction. As it bends the opposite way, the current flows the opposite way. The frequency of this alternating current will be the same as the frequency of the vibrating sound source; thus an electrical analog of an acoustic event has been created.

When we "turn up" the volume of an audio device, we are simply increasing the voltage. One control that allows us to do this is called *voltage potentiometer*, commonly referred to as a *pot*.

Now that we understand how sound waves are converted into electricity, let's examine a common audio system in which our "electrical analog" is put to use: a *public address* (PA) system. A PA system is a way of making sound louder (amplification). The basic components of a common PA system are: a microphone, a pre-amplifier, a power amplifier, a loudspeaker, and cables to connect each of these devices in sequence.

Because the electrical current generated by a microphone is very small it must be increased (amplified) significantly before most audio devices can use it. The microphone must therefore be plugged into a *pre-amplifier*. The pre-amplifier (like all amplifiers) *boosts* the voltage (amplitude) of the electrical signal. The amount of voltage generated by a microphone is known as *mic level*; the pre-amplifier boosts this mic level to a stronger signal, known as *line level*.

Once the electrical signal has been boosted by the pre-amp, it can proceed to the *power amplifier*. The power amplifier's job is to boost the line level signal to an even greater level, known as *speaker level*. It takes a very large amount of electricity (compared to that generated by a pre-amp) to make a typical

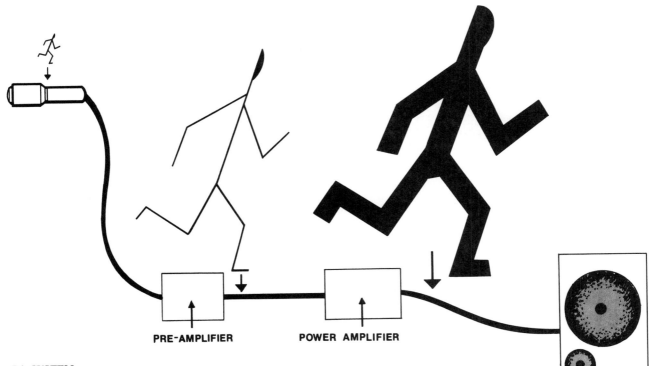

PRE-AMPLIFIER   **POWER AMPLIFIER**   **LOUDSPEAKER**

PA SYSTEM

This simplified illustration of a PA (public address) system shows the three basic levels of electrical signal used in audio work. The PA system amplifies the sounds picked up by the mic, so that they can be heard by many people. It takes two devices to do this: the pre-amplifier boosts the signal from *mic level* up to *line level*; then the power amplifier boosts the line level signal up to *speaker level*. A similar process occurs whenever we listen to sounds coming from microphones, turntables or tape recorders.

loudspeaker work. The speaker level signal can then be sent from the power amplifier to the loudspeaker, where the "analog process" is reversed, and electricity is converted back to sound.

What our simple diagram of a PA system describes is a *gain structure*. The word *gain* in electronics means, simply, a change in volume. Our PA system has two stages of gain. First, the mic level signal is boosted to line level, then the line level signal is boosted to speaker level. The "path" of the signal through all of these components (or through any audio device) is called a *channel*.

KEY TERMS TO REMEMBER

alternating current
amplification
amplitude
analog
channel
conductor
diaphragm
gain
gain structure

intensity
line level
mic level
pot
pre-amplifier
public address (PA) system
signal
speaker level
voltage

ANALOG AND DIGITAL

Digital equipment is becoming more common in audio production each year. Most experts agree that eventually nearly all audio signal storage and processing will be done digitally. In this chapter, first we will describe the basic difference between *analog* and *digital* systems in the simplest possible terms. Secondly, we will discuss the specific relative merits of the two processing systems.

Once a sound has been changed into electricity it can be stored, processed, or transmitted in two basic ways, either as an analog or digital representation.

Have you ever photocopied your face? A photograph of any kind is an analog of its subject. That means it is a representation of something, a representation which is consciously made to be similar to the thing it imitates in some ways though it may be different in others. A photocopy of someone's face, for example, certainly will represent that face in some aspects. But it only exists in two dimensions. It can't change expressions, or laugh, or do anything except be a static copy of some visual characteristics of that person's face.

A black and white photocopy of something like a face will contain many shades of gray. If someone wants a copy of our photocopied face, we can put the original one into a machine and make a copy of it. The quality of the reproduction will noticeably deteriorate between the original document and the first generation copy. After just a few generations the image will look awful. This is a classic problem with analog reproduction. The "noise" and "distortion" inherent in the system we are using will degrade our "signal."

It is those shades of gray that are our real problem. A photocopy machine just isn't very good at duplicating them without adding its "visual noise" in the process.

Here is an alternate scheme. Since the photocopy of the face is made of shades of gray from white to black, let's represent each of those shades of gray with a number. "0" can be white, "1" can be very light gray, "2" can be slightly darker gray, etc. all the way to "10" which can be black. We can alter our photocopy machine so that what it will produce is not an actual photograph but instead is a sheet of paper on which the shade of gray on each point of the face will be represented by a number.

Photocopy machines are very good at reproducing images of numbers because the numbers themselves have no gray in them. The number is black and the paper surrounding the number is white. We can go through many generations of copies of our "number picture" with very little degradation of quality. At any generation we can stop and get our machine to translate the numbers back into the shades of gray that will make a photograph.

Numbers are digits. This alternate scheme would be a form of digital reproduction. In audio, digital reproduction happens in a similar way. Instead of shades of gray, it is voltages that are represented by numbers. Instead of a number system that has 0 through 9, (a "decimal" system) we use a system with only 0 and 1 (a "binary" system). Having only two digits doesn't mean we can't represent large numbers. 1111100101000111101001 is a very large number, but as you can see it can be written with only two kinds of digits.

All of the basic attributes of a sound, its frequency, volume, and duration can be represented by a series of numbers which signify a changing voltage over a period of time.

So this is the basic difference between analog and digital. What are the relative merits of each for audio work today?

Digital audio devices are still much more expensive than their analog counterparts. The quality of work that a digital device will do depends entirely upon the number of digits (bits) it can handle. There are several incompatible professional digital audio tape recorder systems on the market, which makes choosing between them something of a problem.

It is critical to avoid overloading (clipping) a digital signal. The kind of distortion which results is far worse than that which happens when an analog signal is overloaded. Since there is more dynamic range in a digital device than in an analog device, it is advisable to use some of that range and to record, or process, digital signals at lower levels. You should do lots of experimentation with a digital audio recorder, for example, in order to get a feel for acceptable levels without distortion.

But that is about where the disadvantages of digital systems end, and their superiority to analog systems becomes evident. The best digital equipment will out-perform the best analog equipment in terms of signal-to-noise ratio, will do slightly better in terms of distortion, and will be roughly equal in frequency response. Though there is still quite a lot of debate about the last two factors.

Operating digital audio equipment is not fundamentally different from operating analog equipment. The digital part of the device is typically hidden from the user.

Tape editing can be done slightly more accurately with digital recorders, but two machines are required. At this point, two very expensive machines.

DIGITAL FORMATS

As of this writing there are five primary digital audio recording formats:

- *DASH*, which stands for Digital Audio with Stationary Head, comes in 2 track, 24 track, and 48 track. With the exception of Sony's 3402 2 track machine, this format is not razor blade editable; any editing must be done through a computer.

- *PD*, which stands for Professional Digital, comes in 2 and 32 track forms. It can be edited with a razor blade.

- *1610/1630*—These are formats devised by Sony which allow digital audio to be recorded on video tape. No more than 2 tracks can be recorded.

- *PCM-F1*—This is another system for recording digital audio on video tape. It also is limited to 2 tracks.

- *RDAT* (Rotary head Digital Audio Tape)—This is another 2 track format. It doesn't use video tape, but it borrows some of its operational characteristics from video recorders. The record/playback head spins (rotates) as the tape moves over it.

The RDAT format is the only system which can be carried "over the shoulder." The DASH and PD formats are used mostly in music recording studios. The 1610, 1630, and F1 formats are used primarily to record 2 track mixdowns from DASH, PD, or analog 24 track formats.

RDAT is currently limited in its professional applications by the fact that time code cannot easily be recorded on an RDAT machine. It must also be transferred (dubbed) to another format in order to be edited.

DIGITAL AUDIO WORK STATIONS

Once a sound has been converted into a digital signal, it can be processed (edited, made into a "loop," equalized, mixed, etc.) with results even better than are possible with analog. The generic name for the device used to do this kind of work is the Digital Audio Work Station. As of this writing, DAWS are expensive, at least twice as expensive as analog equipment which would do the same kind of work. But the price is bound to come down. Eventually we will all be working with DAWS.

The currently prevailing format for recording the digital audio in a DAWS is a hard, magnetic disk. It looks a little like a phonograph record. A head, similar to a tape recorder head, moves across the spinning disk, recording and playing back information. The generic term for this kind of disk is a Winchester. It is the same kind of disk used in many personal computers.

KEY TERMS TO REMEMBER

analog	digital
binary	digital audio work station
bit	PD
byte	RDAT
DASH	

CHAPTER FIVE

INPUTS AND OUTPUTS

Most audio devices have both *inputs* and *outputs*. Trying to plug an electrical signal into an output will work about as well as trying to force a stream of water back into a gushing hydrant. Whenever any two audio devices are connected certain rules of connection come into play.

There are three important variables which determine whether any two audio devices can be connected:

■ *Level* of output and input

■ *Impedance* of output and input

■ Whether the output and input are *balanced* or *unbalanced*.

Let's take a closer look at each of these three variables.

LEVEL MATCHING

Both inputs and outputs come in all three basic levels: *microphone level, line level,* or *speaker level.* The science of connecting the correct level output with the correct level input is called *level matching.* The general rules are as follows:

■ Mic level outputs *must* be plugged into a pre-amplifier before they can be connected to any other devices. Some tape machines have pre-amps in them. These machines have inputs specifically labelled "MIC" or "MICROPHONE," which means that these particular inputs lead to a pre-amplifier before they go anywhere else inside the device. If the tape machine you plan to use doesn't have a microphone input, then you must find some device which contains a pre-amp, plug your mic into it, and then plug the output of that device into the tape machine. Most mixing consoles will have pre-amps built into them.

■ Line level outputs carry electrical signals which have *already* been pre-amplified. (So don't plug a line level output into a mic level input!) Line level outputs are *only* meant to be connected to line level inputs.

■ Speaker level outputs are *only* meant to be connected to loudspeakers. The signals are much greater than line level signals, and a whole lot greater than mic level signals. Only a power amplifier will generate speaker level signals.

IMPEDANCE MATCHING

All electrical circuits present a certain amount of *resistance* to the flow of electricity through them. The total amount of this opposition in any AC circuit is referred to as the *impedance* of that circuit. To obtain the most efficient transfer of energy from one circuit to another circuit, the impedances of the two circuits should be the same. Impedance in AC circuits (commonly abbreviated "Z") and resistance in DC circuits are both measured in *ohms* (Ω). All inputs and outputs have a given impedance. Matching the *level* of an input to an output does not necessarily result in an impedance match.

If there is an impedance mismatch between two devices, at least one of several things will happen:

- There will be little or no transfer of electricity from one device to the other.

- The level of electricity transferred from the output of one device to the input of the other will be significantly less or greater than would be optimal.

- Certain frequencies of the signal being transferred may be reduced or amplified out of natural proportion to other frequencies within that signal. (If severe, this "frequency response" problem may result in unacceptable tone coloration.)

- Equipment damage may result.

There are devices which can be installed between two pieces of audio equipment which will artificially match their impedances.

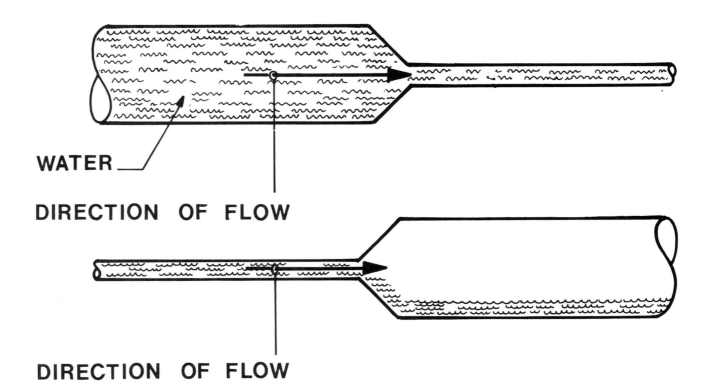

WATER

DIRECTION OF FLOW

DIRECTION OF FLOW

IMPEDANCE MISMATCHES

The large diameter pipe represents a low impedance (low Z), and the small diameter pipe represents a high impedance (high Z). This simple analogy shows that a low impedance output can supply enough electricity for a high impedance input, but a high impedance output just can't give a low impedance input all it needs. Thus, feeding a low impedance output into a high impedance input will often work, but the opposite will not.

The principles of impedance are very complex, and a complete discussion is beyond the scope of this book. But there is one generalization about impedance matching that is simple, and true enough of the time to make it useful to remember: *Usually, an output should have an impedance which is equal to or lower than the impedance into which it is to be plugged.*

This generalization doesn't apply to connecting power amplifiers to speakers. Impedances of amplifier outputs and loudspeakers vary widely—the most common being four, eight and sixteen ohms—and it is critical to have an exact impedance match between amp and speaker, or damage to one or both may occur. If the impedance of either the amp or the speaker is not clearly labeled, do *not* assume you can make a safe connection unless this is verified by a qualified person.

When two audio devices are connected to each other the connection is usually made by means of a cable of some kind. In the world of audio a cable consists of two or more wires that are bound together inside an insulating outer skin.

If we look at a microphone, for instance, there must be at least two wires which extend from that microphone to the device into which it is plugged. At a given instant one of the wires will be conducting the electrical current "away" from the mic, and the other wire will be "returning" it to the mic. Both of the wires are contained inside one cable.

If there are only *two* wires which make the connection between two audio devices, then that connection is said to be *unbalanced*. This is the kind of circuit usually found in non-professional, "consumer" home hi-fi/stereo equipment.

A *balanced* connection between two audio devices necessitates *three* wires running from one device to the other—though a three-wire connection doesn't mean that the circuit is necessarily balanced. Balanced circuits are usually preferable to unbalanced circuits. Balanced circuits are wired so that spurious, unwanted electrical noises tend to cancel themselves out, and so have much less chance of being added to the desired signal. Since a balanced circuit requires more wiring and electrical components than an unbalanced circuit, it is more expensive to make.

Balanced outputs *cannot* be plugged into unbalanced inputs (or vice versa) without special cables. Whenever two devices are to be connected which are not normally connected someone better figure out whether the outs and ins are balanced or unbalanced.

BALANCED AND UNBALANCED CONNECTIONS

KEY TERMS TO REMEMBER

balanced connection
circuit
direct box
impedance
impedance matching transformer

input
ohm
output
unbalanced connection

CHAPTER SIX

STEREO/MONO: WHAT'S THE DIFFERENCE?

This chapter should eliminate a lot of the confusion about what is stereo and what is mono and how to best use each technique. A *stereo* piece of material is one which can be played through two identically calibrated speakers such that the sound coming from one speaker will be different from the sound coming from the other. A *mono* signal, if sent to those same two speakers, will always sound exactly the same coming from either.

The word "stereo" is sometimes used to refer to a recording which is attempting to simulate, more or less, the way our two ears perceive events in the three dimensions of the space around us, principally on the horizontal axis (left/right).

Many recordings which are put on the two adjacent tracks of a tape recorder do not at all represent a *stereo field* as described above. Rather, they simply have a different set of sounds on one track than they have on the other. If I am interviewing you, I may choose to record my voice primarily on one track of a two-track recorder, and your voice on the other. At some later time our voices will probably be mixed onto a single track. But it can be convenient to make the initial recording in two-track "stereo" form so that our voices are more isolated, and can be more easily processed individually later on.

This means that all stereo recordings must have at least two tracks, but all two-track recordings are not necessarily "stereo." I can easily record exactly the same signal on both tracks of a two-track machine. Then I would have a mono recording in two-track format, or *two-track mono*. Usually the only reason to do this is in case there is a *dropout* on one track which does not happen on the other. For example, a small piece of dirt may cover most of one track for an instant, causing the dropout where nothing is recorded, but not affect the other track at all.

When *dubbing* (making a second recording) from a two-track mono recording you should use only one of the tracks. If you combine the two onto a new, single, track there is a greater chance that some frequencies will be cancelled out because of phase errors between the two original tracks. So, dub from either the right or the left track, and if there is a dropout just start over again at the most convenient spot and begin dubbing from the other track. Unfortunately, the dropout may be on both original tracks; but often it will be at

STEREO/TWO TRACK

least slightly less problematic on one or the other. (For a full discussion of phase cancellation see chapter 20.)

IS STEREO BETTER THAN MONO?

Who knows? Is color better than black and white? I recommend that novices not try to do much in stereo until they have exhausted the possibilities of mono.

KEY TERMS TO REMEMBER

dropout

dubbing

mono

stereo

two-track mono

PRIMARY AUDIO DEVICES

This section looks at devices which are basic to audio production since they enable us to process sound by converting it to electrical or magnetic signals.

M ETERS

T he section on the decibel explained that one of the reasons we use decibels to compare levels and loudness in audio is the need to be precise. Real precision in comparing levels of sound, or calibrating a tape recorder to work properly, or lots of other jobs in audio would be impossible without meters.

A meter gives a visual indication of the intensity of an audio signal. It can warn us that we are attempting to record too strong a signal on a tape recorder, or that the signal is so weak that it may be obliterated by noise in our recording system. It can allow us to exactly measure the performance of each of the tape recorders in a studio to make sure that a recording made on one of the machines will sound the same if it is played back on another.

PEAK METERS AND VU METERS

The two basic kinds of meters we commonly find in audio are peak meters and VU meters.

Peak meters respond very quickly to signals which pass through them, and give a very accurate indication of the highest or peak level of the signal. They are most useful if we are concerned about the distortion that may result from a very intense, though very brief, electrical impulse.

VU meters respond more slowly to the signals which pass through them. They are useful if we are concerned with comparing average signal levels (rather than peaks), and specifically they are most useful in comparing how loud to the human ear one sound will be compared to another. Human hearing is more attuned to average levels than to peak levels.

Whether a meter has a needle or is made of a series of lights has nothing to do with whether it is a peak meter or a VU meter. Either kind of meter can take either form.

METERS AND THE "WORKING RANGE"

The dynamic range of sound we encounter in the world and are able to perceive encompasses over 130 decibels. But it is impossible, even with the latest equipment, to effectively record or reproduce it. It's probably good that we can't, since the results could be pretty painful for the audience.

Nearly all of the material we deal with in audio work occupies a much more restricted range of loudness. The dynamic range of a full symphony orchestra performance is rarely more than 80 decibels. That means there is 80dB difference in loudness between the quietest perceivable sound and the loudest. There may be quieter sounds happening, but the audience, even the audience

VU METER

VU meters are good indicators of how loud (to the human ear) one sound will be compared with another. Peak meters, on the other hand, respond more quickly to audio signals and are therefore more useful for monitoring transient (short duration) signals which can cause distortion, and which may pass through a VU meter undetected. Either kind of meter can use a needle or a series of lights.

in the concert hall, will not hear them because of the slight roar of the ventilation system in the room and other ambient noises which constitute the *noise floor* of the environment.

A rock-n-roll concert is likely to have much less dynamic range, 20 or 30dB. Remember that we are not talking about "absolute loudness" but rather the RANGE of loudness, from top to bottom.

Most of the time, no matter what medium we are working in, the *dynamic range* of the signals with which we are working is within 30 or 40 decibels. Most of the notes and chords of a symphony are within 30 decibels of each other.

Our medium, our audio recording and/or reproduction system, also has a certain dynamic range. It has a noise floor, and it has an upper limit beyond which any signal will be distorted. The challenge is somehow to fit our *acoustic event* with its dynamic range into our audio medium with its dynamic range. The usual approach is to feed the event into the system such that the loudest sound will be just a few decibels below the threshold where distortion will occur.

This will mean that most of the signal levels will be between 0 and 30 decibels below that threshold of distortion. Since that is the range of levels we will be dealing with most often, it is also the range we will be most interested in metering. That is why most of the meters we use only monitor a range of about 30dB very effectively. In fact, the meter is usually most sensitive to an even smaller range which corresponds to approximately 20dB below the onset of distortion.

KEY TERMS TO REMEMBER

acoustic event
dynamic range

noise floor

M CHAPTER EIGHT
ICROPHONES

There is an incredible amount of mythology surrounding the use of mics. It is best to avoid assuming a particular mic is best for a certain application until you've made lots of comparisons yourself. By all means don't forget that the positioning of a microphone is extremely important in determining what sound you will get. A good recordist will spend a lot more time thinking about and experimenting with the position of the mic than he or she will spend deciding what mic to use.

One naive assumption is that some microphones are for "music" recording, and some are for "voice" recording. The human voice is capable of producing an extremely wide spectrum of sound, and should not be short-changed. As an experiment, record someone speaking. Use a high quality studio mic, and make as good a recording as possible. Now play back that recording through an equalizer and filter out whatever part of the audio spectrum you choose. You will probably find that any frequency you remove between 60 Hertz and 15,000 Hertz will be missed as much as if it had been removed from most "musical instruments" recorded similarly.

We will be dealing here with "professional" microphones which are commonly used in broadcasting and recording. They range in price from $50 to $2000, and come in many sizes and shapes.

Microphones are categorized in four basic ways:

■ by their method of generating electricity from sound

■ by their directional characteristics

■ by their frequency response

■ by their application

METHODS OF GENERATING ELECTRICITY FROM SOUND

The part of a microphone which actually turns sound into electricity is called the *element*. There are three basic types of elements: *dynamic*, *ribbon* and *condenser*.

DYNAMIC MICROPHONES

Dynamic mics, also called *moving coil mics*, contain a diaphragm attached to a coil of wire. This coil of wire is located within the magnetic field of a permanent magnet, also inside the microphone.

When sound waves strike the diaphragm, which lies just inside the wire mesh screen of most mics, the diaphragm vibrates back and forth. This causes the coil of wire to move back and forth through the magnetic field. As we have said, when an electrical conductor (like our coil of wire) moves through a magnetic field, an electrical current is generated which flows through that conductor.

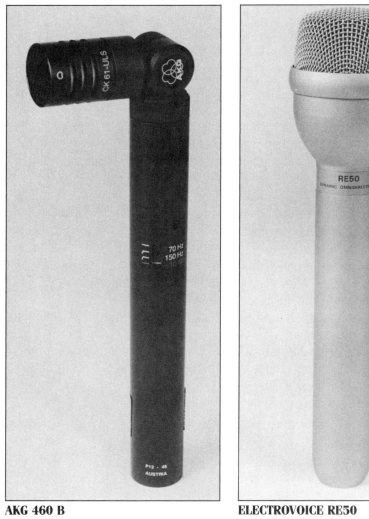

AKG 460 B

The 460, like its predecessor the 451, has an interchangeable capsule to the body of the mic. The version pictured here has a swivel between the capsule and body.

ELECTROVOICE RE50

The Electrovoice RE 50 is probably the mic most often used by reporters. It is rugged, and relatively immune to handling noise and wind problems.

RIBBON MICROPHONES

Ribbon microphones work according to the same principles as dynamic microphones. Both types use an internal magnet. The difference between the two is that the ribbon mic uses a single corrugated strip (ribbon) of metal as its moving element, while the dynamic mic uses a diaphragm and coil. The ribbon vibrates within the magnetic field and so generates electricity.

CONDENSER MICROPHONES

The word *condenser* is an old name for the electrical device which is now called a *capacitor*. A capacitor consists of two plates which are separated by a non-conductor (a substance which does not conduct electricity). One of these plates is flexible.

A constant electrical charge is maintained within each plate, and an electrical relationship exists between the two plates. (This charge is provided by a separate power source, sometimes a battery within the microphone itself.) When sound waves strike the movable plate, the electrical relationship between the two plates is changed, and a current is caused to flow.

NEUMANN U-87

The Neumann U-87 is a widely used microphone in studio music and voice recording work. Its directional characteristics are switchable between omni-, bi-, and uni-directional.

DIRECTIONAL CHARACTERISTICS OF MICS

Another way in which microphones are categorized is by their effectiveness in reproducing sounds from various directions. Different types of microphones have different "directional characteristics." The *axis* of a microphone is a straight line drawn from the mic in the direction it will be best able to respond to incoming sounds.

There are three general "patterns" of directional characteristics of microphones: *omnidirectional*, *bidirectional*, and *unidirectional*.

OMNIDIRECTIONAL

An omnidirectional microphone is one that is designed to be nearly equally sensitive to sounds coming from all directions. The pattern of an "omni" mic is usually described as circular. Actually, of course, it's spherical.

A *lavalier* mic is a specialized kind of *omni mic*, small enough to hang around the neck or attach to clothing. They are most useful in cases where larger mics would seem obtrusive. Recently some directional lavaliers have become available, but they are not used very widely.

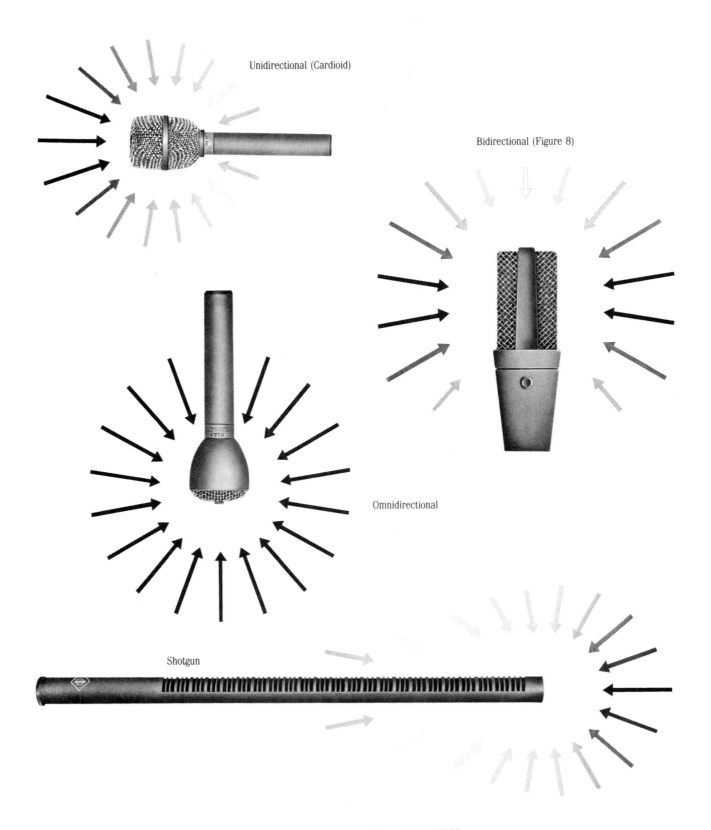

Unidirectional (Cardioid)

Bidirectional (Figure 8)

Omnidirectional

Shotgun

DIRECTIONAL CHARACTERISTICS OF MICS

The four most basic directional response patterns of microphones: unidirectional (cardioid); bidirectional (figure 8); omnidirectional; and shotgun. The darker arrows indicate a greater sensitivity to sound.

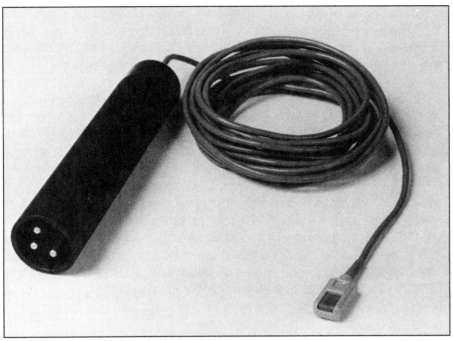

TRAM LAVALIER MICROPHONE

The microphone is the tiny capsule on the right of the photo. Its three-pin connector on the left of the picture is a normal size mic plug, which indicates the small size of this omni-directional microphone.

BIDIRECTIONAL

A bidirectional microphone is one that is designed to respond best to sounds coming from only two specific directions. The pickup pattern of a bidirectional mic is a figure 8 (or in three dimensions, a dumbbell).

UNIDIRECTIONAL

A unidirectional microphone is one that responds well to sounds coming from only one specific direction. The pickup pattern of a "uni" mic is described as cardioid (heart-shaped). However, cardioid mics do not by any means completely reject *off-axis* sounds. They merely reduce the volume of these sounds in proportion to *on-axis* sounds. And, as we will see, in some mics the off-axis frequency response is not flat—not accurately reproduced.

FREQUENCY RESPONSE

The "frequency response" of a microphone refers to how well a particular mic is able to respond to all the frequencies of sound waves which strike it. A microphone which is able to reproduce any given range of frequencies accurately is said to have *flat* frequency response in that range.

Most high-quality professional microphones have reasonably flat *response over most of the range of frequencies that people can hear—the audio range* (16-20,000 Hz). Some mics, however, do not accurately reproduce low frequencies, while others do not accurately reproduce high frequencies.

Practically all of the sound sources which we record contain frequencies throughout the entire audio range. If we use a microphone which has flat response only from 100 to 4,000 Hz to record a piano, for instance, the result will be easily identifiable as a piano, but the full range of frequencies which the piano produces will not be heard on the tape.

Or, to use a different example: if intelligibility is our only aim in making a recording of a human voice, then a very cheap microphone (like that in a telephone) is all we need. But if we want to make a recording which will accurately reproduce the sound of a human voice *as we would hear it in person*, then a mic with flat response from at least 100 to 15,000 Hz is necessary.

The two main variables which affect frequency response in microphones are the *type* of microphone used (i.e., dynamic, ribbon or condenser) and the *placement* of the microphone with relation to the sound source. In general, good condenser mics have more accurate frequency response than dynamic or ribbon mics. Good ribbon mics are most prized for voice recording. Traditionally, male announcers have used ribbon mics because of the tendency of ribbon microphones to enhance bass frequencies. Many people feel that ribbon mics produce a "warmer" sound than other mics.

AKG C 414 B

This high quality condenser mic is switchable between cardioid, hypercardioid, omni, and figure eight patterns. It also has a switchable pad and bass roll-off.

Dynamic mics fall within two general categories in terms of frequency response. There are those with relatively flat response from about 100 to 12,000 Hz and those (more expensive) with flat response from 50 to 15,000 Hertz.

A phenomenon which occurs with all microphones to some extent, and with uni-directional microphones in particular is *proximity effect*. Whenever a microphone is placed very close to a sound source (less than six inches), there is a tendency for the low frequencies to be boosted out of proportion to the high frequencies. Certain cardioid microphones are designed to keep proximity effect at a minimum; these mics are especially useful in PA system work and other situations requiring particularly close miking.

Up to this point, we have been speaking about *on-axis* or "on-mic" frequency response—the response of microphones to sound sources specifically within their pickup pattern. However, microphones also differ in their *off-axis* or "off-mic" frequency response.

We have already seen that even the most directional of mics will not completely reject off-axis sounds which strike it. When a microphone with a poor off-axis frequency response picks up an off-axis sound, it will tend to emphasize certain frequencies over others, which can result in a "tinny" or a "muffled" effect. This is known as *coloration*.

Off-axis discoloration can occur when there are many mics in a relatively small space, each assigned to a different sound source. Each of the mics will inevitably pick up at least a little of *all* of the nearby sources. When we combine the outputs of all those mics, the total "mix" of sound we hear may be noticeably discolored, due to the indirect, off-axis sounds.

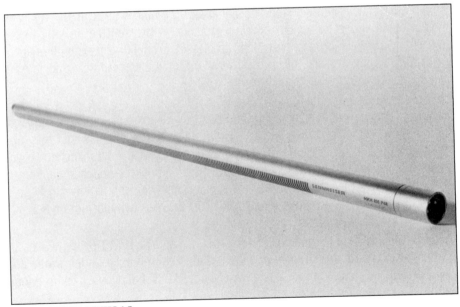

SENNHEISER MKH816

The Sennheiser MKH 816 is used for film and television production around the world. It is highly directional, but has poor off-axis frequency response when compared to less directional mics.

Another source of off-axis discoloration is the reflection of sounds from walls, floors, ceilings and objects inside a room. The original sound source may be on-axis to the microphone, but the reflected sound (also picked up by that mic) will be off-axis and, in a mic with poor off-axis frequency response, discolored.

All of the above discussion should make one important point clear: the largest single factor which determines the frequency response of a particular mic in a particular situation is *the placement of the mic in relation to the sound source it is supposed to pick up!* If a microphone is too close, too far, or off-axis in relation to its sound source, frequency response will suffer. These factors will tend to have a much greater effect (in terms of frequency response) than the kind of mic used.

OTHER MICS YOU SHOULD KNOW

Among the types of microphones we haven't mentioned specifically there are five that are noteworthy:

PZM (pressure zone) microphones are designed to be placed on floors, walls, tables or ceilings. They usually consist of a small, omni-directional element mounted just barely above the surface of a hard, flat plate. The principal advantage of this kind of mount is that it eliminates one source of reflected sound from the acoustic field in which it sits. If a mic can't be placed close to a given sound source, and if the desire is to reduce some of the acoustic reverberation in the room then a PZM might be worth a try. Any omni mic, if placed less than an inch from a floor, ceiling, table or wall will probably yield a similar effect. Directional PZM's are also available.

"Contact" mics are designed to be physically attached to a vibrating object. Unlike other mics, contact mics do not pick up sound waves in the air. The motion of the object to which they are attached is transmitted directly to the mic which converts it to electrical impulses. Aside from being used with musical instruments they are also often used in sound effects recording, especially to record the vibration of metallic objects.

Binaural mics are designed to simulate the directional characteristics of human ears. These mics are always stereo, just like our ears. In fact they are often mounted inside the "ears" of a plastic model of a human head. To get the proper effect of binaural recording one must listen to it through headphones. If done properly the effect can be astonishing, allowing the listener to hear a sound source appear to move in a circle, 360 degrees around him or her.

A hydrophone is designed to be submersible, and picks up sound waves in water and other liquids. Nearly any microphone can be used under water if it is protected by a waterproof covering of some kind, but using a hydrophone will avoid the risk of ruining an "air" mic.

So-called "parabolic" mics are actually just normal mics that have been placed in the "focus" of a parabolic dish. The effect of the dish is to make the microphone extremely uni-directional. The disadvantage of this technique is that the response of the parabolic mic to low frequencies is limited by the diameter of the dish. It isn't very practical to carry around a dish larger than three feet or so, and at three feet there will be no response to frequencies below approximately three hundred Hertz.

For some recording, low frequency response is not important. Ornithologists, for example, use parabolic mics to record bird vocalizations. Very few birds generate frequencies lower than three hundred Hertz, vocally.

As we have said earlier, all microphones generate very low level electrical signals (mic level), which must be pre-amplified to line level before other audio equipment can use them.

MIC LEVEL, PRE-AMPLIFIERS, AND "CLIPPING"

Most pre-amps have a fixed amount of *gain* or amplification. This means that all input signals fed into them are amplified the same amount. Some pre-amps, however, have a control which allows one to vary the gain.

Most condenser mics generate a "hotter" or higher level of electricity than either dynamic or ribbon mics. In addition, microphones of the same type will generate different amounts of electricity depending on the volume of the sound source they are picking up—the louder the sound source, the stronger the electrical signal. At times, the signal can be so strong as to *overload* the input of a fixed-gain pre amp, which will tend to over-amplify this already strong signal.

This is a common source of distortion when recording any loud sounds. Severe distortion of this kind produces a "crackling" sound during the loudest portions of the passage. The signal in this case is said to have been "clipped." For this reason, it is best to use variable-gain pre-amps whenever possible, so that it is possible to lower the amount of pre-amp gain when using "hot" condenser mics, or when a particularly loud sound is expected.

If a variable-gain pre-amp is not available when needed, a simple device called a *pad* can be inserted between the mic output and the pre-amp input. A pad attenuates (reduces the level of) the mic output signal by a specific amount (usually 10, 15, 20 or 25 dB). Some microphones have built-in pads, which can be switched in or out of the circuit. The reduction in level is usually accomplished by sending the signal through a network of resistors which lower its voltage.

Quite a lot of the signal distortion that happens when using microphones is a result of mic pre-amp clipping. Adjusting the volume control on the tape recorder or mixing console will not reduce this kind of distortion because the distorted signal is created before the signal even gets to those controls. Some tape recorders have a switchable pad which can reduce the input signal by 20 decibels.

The differences among high quality, professional microphones are not nearly as great as we might assume at first glance. The *way* in which we use this equipment is the most important factor in successful production work. With this in mind, here are some general considerations in choosing a microphone:

GENERAL CONSIDERATIONS IN CHOOSING MICROPHONES

DYNAMIC MICS:

■ Are very durable

■ Can be omni- or unidirectional

- Will emphasize bass frequencies if the sound source is with in a few inches of the mic (proximity effect). This is especially true of cardioid mics.
- Do not require a power supply.

RIBBON MICS:

- Are sometimes delicate
- Are usually bidirectional
- Have generally good on- and off-axis frequency response
- Don't require a power supply
- Cannot be used in wind

CONDENSER MICS:

- Are delicate
- Can be omni- and/or uni- and/or bidirectional
- Require a power supply (battery or external)
- Have excellent frequency response and transient response
- Have a higher output level than dynamic or ribbon mics.

KEY TERMS TO REMEMBER

axis of microphone	lavalier mic
bidirectional mic	moving coil mic
capacitor	off-axis
cardioid mic	omnidirectional mic
clipping	on-axis
close miking	pad
condenser mic	pickup pattern
directional characteristics	plosive consonants
discoloration	popping
dynamic mic	proximity effect
element	ribbon mic
figure 8 mic	shotgun mic
flat frequency response	transient response
gain	unidirectional mic

CHAPTER NINE

TAPE MACHINES

Most professional tape machines perform two primary tasks: 1) recording audio signals on tape; and 2) reproducing (playing back) signals stored on tape.

There are three types of tape machines: *reel-to-reel* (or *open reel*), *cart*, and *cassette*. The basic method of storing and retrieving magnetic impulses on tape, however, is the same in all three.

In the section on electricity, we learned that whenever a conductor is moved through a magnetic field an electrical current is generated. Likewise, whenever an electrical current flows through a conductor, a magnetic field is generated around the conductor. If a magnetizable substance, such as iron, is placed within this field, it becomes a temporary magnet for as long as there is current flowing. This is referred to as an *electromagnet*.

HOW AN ANALOG TAPE MACHINE RECORDS

After an electrical audio signal enters a tape recorder, it is sent to the *recording head*. This is actually two pieces of metal, separated by a tiny gap over which the tape slides. Two wires are attached to the recording head, making it a part of the same circuit that began at the microphone. The head itself is simply a small electromagnet. The current which powers this electromagnet is the very same signal generated by our microphone.

The magnetic tape which slides over the recording head is a strip of very thin plastic, coated on one side with some magnetizable substance.

As the tape passes over our electromagnet (the recording head), the pulses of magnetism generated by the audio signal powering the head magnetize the iron particles on the recording tape. As the signal pulses in one direction, it creates one tiny "magnet" on the tape. As it pulses in the other direction it creates a second, oppositely-polarized "magnet" on the tape.

Since the tape is moving past the recording head, each new pulse from the head will magnetize the area of tape just adjacent to the area magnetized by the previous pulse. And since our signal consists of hundreds or more often thousands of these pulses surging back and forth every second (depending on the frequency of the signal), we create along the length of the tape a series of oppositely polarized "magnets." Each of these "magnets" will vary in strength, depending on the intensity (amplitude) of the electrical signal which created it.

Once again we have created an analog. This time it is a *magnetic* analog of an *electrical* signal—which was itself an analog of the sound waves picked up by our microphone.

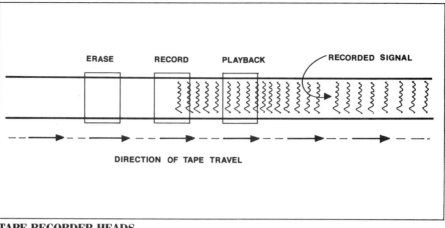

TAPE RECORDER HEADS

This drawing shows the three heads found on professional tape recorders. Notice that since the playback head follows the recording head, it is possible to listen to a recorded sound immediately after it has been recorded and while the recording is still happening. Thus, even while the machine is recording, the "meter-and-output" selector can be switched to "playback," and the signal recorded a split second before can be monitored.

HOW A TAPE MACHINE PLAYS BACK

To listen to (play back) tape which has already been recorded, another head is used to reverse this analog process. The *playback head* is a conductor that converts the *magnetic* impulses which have been "stored" on the tape back into alternating *electrical* impulses.

MULTI-TRACK TAPE HEADS

This photograph shows the erase, record and playback heads of a sixteen-track tape recorder. This sixteen-track format uses tape that is two inches wide.

We have said before that any time an electrical conductor moves through a magnetic field, an electrical current is caused to flow through the conductor. This is precisely what happens when the recorded magnetic impulses on the tape move past the playback head of the tape machine.

That is, as the thousands of individual magnetic fields on the tape pass by the playback head, each of them generates an electrical impulse. Since each "magnet" is oppositely polarized from the previous one, the electrical impulses which they generate surge, or alternate, back and forth. Two wires attached to the playback head complete the circuit connecting the tape machine to whichever audio device we wish to send our signal—for instance, the power amplifier and loudspeakers we discussed in our model PA system.

Ideally, the electrical analog created by the tape passing over the playback head would exactly match the signal we generated with our microphone in frequency and relative amplitude.

Most tape recorders also have an erase head, which serves to "destroy" the magnetic arrangements of a previously recorded tape. The erase head generates a strong electrical signal which makes random the arrangement of magnetic fields along the tape. The erase head is activated whenever the machine is recording; it is usually positioned just before the recording head in the tape path.

It is important to remember that *any* magnetic field can erase or degrade the magnetic arrangement of a recorded tape. Always keep tapes away from any magnetic or electrical sources to protect them from such degradation. Electric power cords, transformers, motors, speakers, amplifiers, and the like *all* generate magnetic fields. Even the weakest magnetic field may be harmful to recorded tape. So watch it!

HOW A TAPE MACHINE ERASES

As we have said, virtually all magnetic tape consists of a strip of plastic backing (usually *polyester*) which is completely covered on one side by tiny particles of some magnetizable *oxide*. The type of oxide used, the thickness of the backing, the width of the tape, and the length of the tape can all vary.

MAGNETIC RECORDING TAPE

TYPES OF OXIDE

There are currently several kinds of magnetizable oxides used in recording tape. The most common is *ferric oxide* (Fe_2O). *Chromium dioxide* (CrO_2) and a *ferro-chromium* (FeCr) combination are also used, especially in cassette recording.

In addition, oxide coatings will vary according to the formulation of the oxide, the density of the coating, and the uniformity of its application. All of these variables will influence the relative price and quality of the tape.

THICKNESS

Thickness of tape is measured in *mils*. One mil is a thousandth of an inch. Most professional recording is done on tape which is 1½ mils thick. Open-

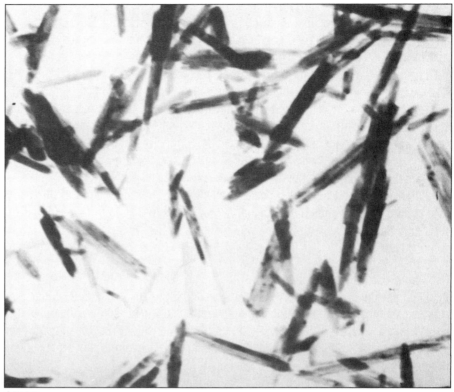

OXIDE

Tiny particles of rust (ferric oxide) magnified 40,000 times. Recording tape is completely covered on one side by these or similar particles that can be magnetized in sequences that represent sounds.

reel tape is also available in 1-mil and ½-mil thicknesses. It is generally preferable to use 1½-mil tape because it is more resistant to stretching or breaking, and because of its resistance to *print-through*.

Print-through occurs when the magnetic impulses on one layer of tape on a reel slightly magnetize the layer immediately above or below it. The thinner the tape the more likely print-through will be a problem. How tightly the tape is wound, how long it is stored, the temperature, and the presence of sun spots may also be factors.

One major misconception about print-through is that it can be reduced by using a lower recording level. This is actually not the case. The ratio between the primary signal and the printed-through signal will remain constant regardless of recording level. Of course, if the recording level is low enough the print-through will be masked by tape hiss or the environmental noise of the listening area, which is probably what fools us into thinking that lowering the recording level is having an effect on the level of the print-through. Lowering the recording level doesn't really get rid of print-through; it only makes the recording noisier.

The ways to avoid print-through are:

■ Leave the tape recording wound tails-out;

■ Use noise reduction (Dolby® or DBX®);

■ Use tape with a thick backing material (at least 1½ mil);

■ Use "low print" tape.

WIDTH

Reel-to-reel audio tape comes in quarter-inch, half-inch, one-inch and two-inch widths. Quarter-inch tape is by far the most widely used. The wider sizes of tape are used for "multi-track" tape machines. Cassette tape is one-eighth inch wide.

LENGTH

The amount (number of feet) of tape on a reel is determined by the size of the reel and the thickness of the tape. The three sizes of reels most commonly used are 5 inches, 7 inches and 10½ inches in diameter.

Another factor which can affect the capacity of a reel is its *hub* size. Most 5-inch and 7-inch reels have "small" hubs (1¾ inches in diameter). Most 10½ inch reels have "large" hubs (5½ inches in diameter). Some 10½ inch reels have a large hole in the center of the hub. These are commonly called *NAB reels*. They require a special *NAB adapter* to fit onto a regular spindle.

It is important to use the same size of reel for supply and take-up. This helps keep the tension of the tape even as it winds onto the take-up reel.

REELS

The most commonly-used reels: 5 inches, 7 inches, and 10½ inches in diameter. A small hole in the center is called an "EIA" hub; the large hole an "NAB" hub.

The amount of recording time available on a full reel of tape is determined by the size of the reel, the thickness of the tape, and the recording speed used. The chart below provides an easy reference.

Thickness	10½ inch reel				7 inch reel				5 inch reel			
	Tape length	Recording time in minutes			Tape length	Recording time in minutes			Tape length	Recording time in minutes		
		15 ips	*7½ ips*	*3¾ ips*		*15 ips*	*7½ ips*	*3¾ ips*		*15 ips*	*7½ ips*	*3¾ ips*
1½ mil	2400 ft	30:00	60:00	120:00	1200 ft	15:00	30:00	60:00	600 ft	7:30	15:00	30:00
1 mil	3600 ft	45:00	90:00	180:00	1800 ft	22:30	45:00	90:00	900 ft	11:15	22:30	45:00
½ mil	4800 ft	60:00	120:00	240:00	2400 ft	30:00	60:00	120:00	1200 ft	15:00	30:00	60:00

RECORDING TIME

Cassette tapes are available in a variety of lengths, ranging from several minutes to two hours of recording time, when recorded in both directions.

Many tape machines have built-in counters which are not really very helpful in production work, since they do *not* correspond to either real time or reel length. Some machines, however, have built-in *tape timers*. They allow us to time a recorded program or to find a particular spot within a reel.

The most accurate tape timers are *digital* (electronic) timers. These can give a "real-time" read-out regardless of which tape speed is used. *Mechanical* timers generally only read real time at one speed, usually *7½ inches per second* (ips). To determine real time at 3¾ ips, simply multiply the timer reading by two; to determine it for 15 ips, divide the timer reading by two. Timers are also very convenient for timing a reel while it is being fast-wound.

If a tape machine does not have a built-in timer, devices are available which can be attached to it. A good tape timer will give a reading within ± 5 seconds of accuracy even at fast-wind speeds. These timers actually measure the physical length of the tape. They convert this length to a readout of how many minutes and seconds it would take to play at normal speed.

CARE OF TAPE

- Always handle tape reels as you handle a phonograph record, i.e., only by the center and edge. Never pinch the sides (flanges) of a reel.

- Whenever possible, avoid using a warped reel. Tape scraping against the flange will be damaged, and the noise it makes will be picked up by any live mic nearby.

- Always store tape in a box, safe from dust.

- Never store a tape *fast-wound*. Always play the tape through at normal, or double normal, speed before storing it for longer than a few hours. There should be no sharp edges of tape sticking up above the other layers. This helps avoid print-through, stretched tape, and crushed edges.

- Never leave a tape in the sunlight, or anywhere the temperature is over eighty degrees or under fifty degrees for more than a few minutes.

■ Keep recorded tapes as far away as possible from all magnets, including those in motors, speakers and bulk erasers.

■ Wash your hands before handling tape. The oil on your fingers will cause dust to stick to the tape, which will result in poor tape/head contact. For this reason, it is important to avoid touching the oxide side of the tape whenever possible.

■ Always label both the reel and the box of any recorded program. You might even consider writing an identification of some kind on the head and tail leader of the tape itself, so that if it gets separated from its original box and reel you will still be able to visually identify it.

REEL-TO-REEL (OPEN REEL) TAPE MACHINES

Almost all professional audio work involves the use of a *reel-to-reel* or *open reel* tape machine. It is called "open reel" because the tape winds from the *supply reel* to the *take-up reel* without being permanently attached to either, and is not enclosed in a cassette or cartridge.

There are several kinds of reel-to-reel tape machines. They are distinguished mostly by the width of the tape they use and by their "track configuration."

TRACK CONFIGURATIONS

Track configuration refers to the number of separate, distinct audio channels that can be recorded on a single tape, and where those signals (*tracks*) are placed on the tape itself.

A mono tape recorder is capable of recording and/or reproducing only one channel of audio. Lots of mics may be sent into a mono machine, but once those signals have been mixed together they cannot be separated.

A "stereo" or two-track machine can handle two distinct channels.

The term "multi-track" usually refers to a machine that can handle four, eight, sixteen, or twenty four channels.

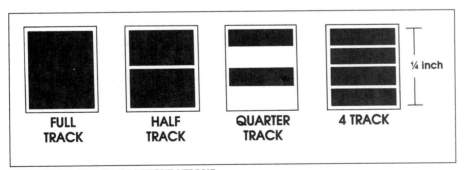

TAPE HEAD TRACK CONFIGURATIONS

The most basic track configuration consists of a single audio signal recorded on the entire width of the tape. This is known as *full-track*. It is, of course, a *mono* signal. The recording head contains a single recording element, which is approximately the same width as the tape. As the tape passes over the recording element, the entire surface of the tape is magnetically imprinted with one audio signal.

Half-track recording is accomplished by a recording head containing *two* separate recording elements each approximately *one-half* the width of the tape. Different audio signals can be sent simultaneously (or successively) to each of the recording elements. Thus, on a half-track tape recorder we can record *two mono signals*, or *one stereo signal* in one direction.

If we want to record *more* than two channels at once, we need a *multi-track* tape recorder. There are many different kinds of multi-track tape recorders used, with varying numbers of recording elements. The following illustration uses the track configuration for a four-track tape recorder as an example.

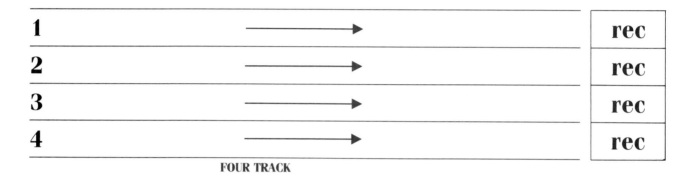

FOUR TRACK

Originally, multi-track recording was mostly used for recording live music to be transferred to phonograph records. Now, though, more audio producers are using multi-track recorders for studio work.

TAPE TRANSPORT

That part of the tape machine which moves the tape from the supply reel across the heads, and onto the take-up reel is called the *transport*.

The major components of the transport are: the reel motors, the tensioners, the tape guides, the capstan and pinch roller, and the transport function controls.

The *reel motors* provide the power to move the tape from one reel to the other in "fast wind" mode. The *tensioners* help maintain a constant tension on the tape, ensuring even pressure as it moves across the heads, and a uniform *pack* as it is wound onto the take-up reel. The *tape guides* also steady the movement of the tape, so that it maintains its correct position relative to the heads.

The tape's speed as it moves past the heads is controlled by the *capstan*, a shaft which rotates at a precise and constant rate of speed. The *pinch roller* holds the tape firmly against the capstan. Since the consistency of the tape's speed depends upon an absolutely even pressure between the capstan and the pinch-roller, it is critical that these parts be kept thoroughly clean.

The *transport function controls* are simply the buttons allowing the operator to control the movement and speed of the tape: fast-winding (forward and

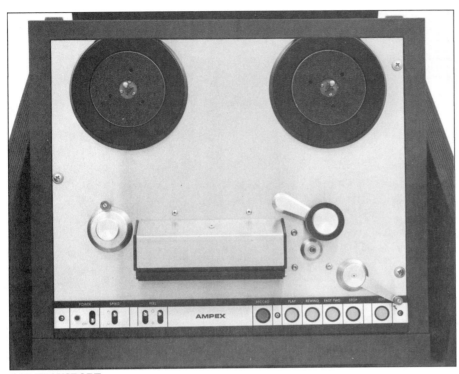

440 TRANSPORT

Though this tape recorder is no longer made, we have chosen to use it to illustrate the basic tape machine functions because its design was simple, lacking the "bells and whistles" which, after all, are of secondary importance.

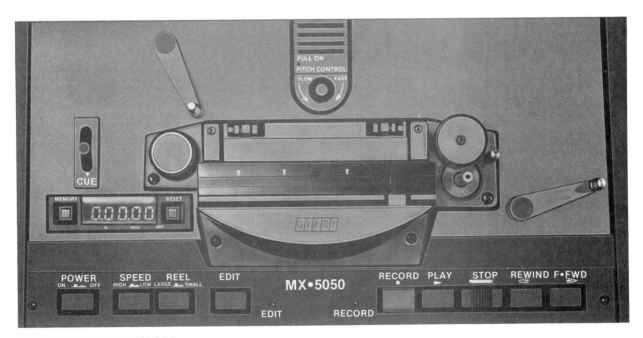

OTARI MX 5050 TRANSPORT

The Otari 5050 is a machine which is widely used today. Some of its features, which older tape recorders like the Ampex 440 did not have, are a continuously variable speed (pitch) control; a tape timer; and an oscillator (tone generator) for machine alignment and level calibration.

440 IN RACK

An Ampex 440 open reel professional studio tape recorder, in "rack mount" format. The basic design is similar to most high quality studio machines. Notice that it is divided into basically two sections. (1) The "electronics" contains the meters, switches, and volume controls that regulate the input and output of signal. (2) The "transport" has the job of conveying the tape and housing the "heads" that actually lay the signal on the tape and pick it up.

rewind), play, stop and pause. Some machines will have additional controls which perform other specialized transport functions.

OPEN REEL TAPE MACHINE

Ampex 440-B tape recorder in a "pedestal mount," a common format for studio work. We know that this machine is mono because it has only one set of "electronics." It may, however, be either "half-track" or "full-track."

TAPE SPEED

Most professional recorders operate at either 7.5 and 15 inches per second (ips) or 15 and 30. Generally speaking, the higher the tape speed, the higher the fidelity. One reason for this is, again, that at a higher speed there is a larger surface area of tape per magnetic impulse, and thus more oxide particles available to store the information.

The higher the speed the less likely that small inconsistencies in the tape surface, including particles of dirt, will be audible. Also, the higher the tape speed the more distance there will be between words, musical notes, etc., making it easier to edit by splicing.

TAPE MACHINE ELECTRONICS

The part of the tape machine which processes the audio signal during recording and playback is called the *electronics*.

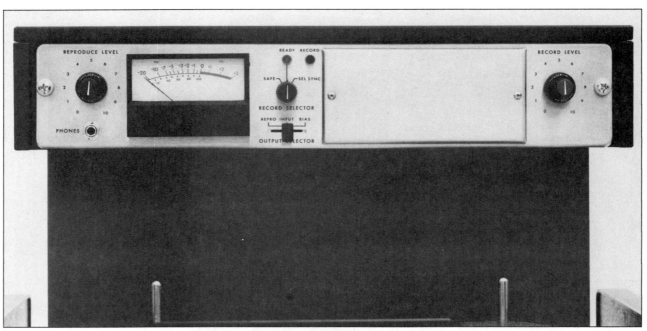

TAPE MACHINE ELECTRONICS, FRONT PANEL

A close-up of the 440 electronics. In the "safe" position of the middle switch the machine will not record even if its record button is pushed accidentally. The "sel sync" position allows for a recorded signal to be played back through the record head rather than the reproduce head as usual. This is useful in "overdubbing." The "output selector" determines whether it will be the signal to be recorded or one which has already been recorded that will appear at the machine's output and be monitored by the VU meter.

The "front panel" of the electronics of most professional tape recorders should contain the following for each channel:

- A *meter-and-output* switch
- A *recording level control*
- A *playback level control*
- A *meter*

Meter-and-Output Switch. This switch usually has two positions. One position, called "Input," "Source," or "Record," allows us to monitor (hear and see on the meter) the incoming signal before it is put on tape.

The other position, called "PLAY," "PLAYBACK," "TAPE," or "REPRODUCE," allows us to monitor the signal which the playback head is picking up *from the tape itself.* When the switch is in this position, the recorded signal from the playback head will be sent to the meter and to the line and headphone outputs of the machine.

This switch does *not* control whether the machine is recording. It simply allows us to compare the signal we want to record ("INPUT") with our own recording of it ("PLAYBACK").

OTARI ELECTRONICS

Recording Level Control. This control determines the level of the incoming signal being sent to the recording head (and to the tape machine's outputs). With the meter-and-output switch in the "SOURCE" position, use the tape recorder's meter to set the proper recording level.

Playback Level Control. This knob controls the level of signal being sent to the tape machine's output from the playback head. With the meter-and-output switch in the "PLAYBACK" position, use the tape recorder's meter to set the proper playback level.

The Volume Unit (VU) Meter. Learning how to read a VU meter is one of the most important parts of your introduction to audio work. It is crucial to the operation of most of the equipment you will be using. A volume unit meter, as the name suggests, measures the volumes of audio signals.

The meter on the tape recorder has two main functions:

■ To indicate the level of the electrical signal being sent to the recording head (and to the machine's output connector) during recording; and

■ To indicate the level of the electrical signal being sent to the machine's output jack during playback.

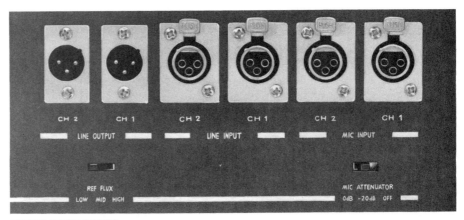

OTARI BACK PANEL

There is a switch on the back of the 5050 electronics which allows a mic level signal coming into the machine to be attenuated 20 dB if it is "loud" enough to cause distortion inside the recorder otherwise.

AVOIDING NOISE AND DISTORTION

A signal that is recorded at too high a level will be distorted. One that is recorded too low in level will be obscured by noise. A major part of the recording technician's job involves trying to reconcile these two facts.

BIAS

In the 1950's, it was found that distortion could be reduced if an ultrasonic (too high in frequency to hear) tone were recorded along with the signal. This tone is called the *bias* tone. Since magnetic tape is manufactured under many different formulas, and since each formulation requires a different level of bias tone, the bias level in each tape machine must also be adjustable.

It is standard procedure to adjust the bias level of a tape machine for the kind of tape which will be used on that machine most often. This is usually an

BIAS SIGNAL AND BIAS ADJUSTMENT CONTROL

Here's a view of the front of the 440 electronics with the metal panel removed that covers the adjustment controls. Every once in a while these screw-headed knobs have to be rotated in order for the general level of the bias, erase, and "audio" signals to be maintained at their optimum intensities.

The most obscure (possibly) of the normally visible controls is the "bias" position of the "output selector." With the switch in this position it is the bias signal that appears on the VU meter and at the output of the electronics. There is only a bias signal, though, when the machine is in the record mode.

internal adjustment, done "on the bench" by a qualified technician. Some tape machines, however, have a bias adjustment that is a front panel control.

TAPE RECORDER EQUALIZATION

The term *equalization* refers to the ability to control the level of any of the frequencies within a given audio signal. Bass and treble tone controls represent a simple form of equalization.

Some equalization is necessary during the recording and playback operations of tape recording in order to compensate for losses of certain frequencies due to the imperfections of the magnetic medium. This equalization is done automatically by the electronics inside the machine, but adjustments by a technician are necessary from time to time.

SELECTIVE SYNCHRONIZATION

Most modern three-head tape recorders have a feature called *selective synchronization* (or simply sync) which allows us to monitor the *playback* signal

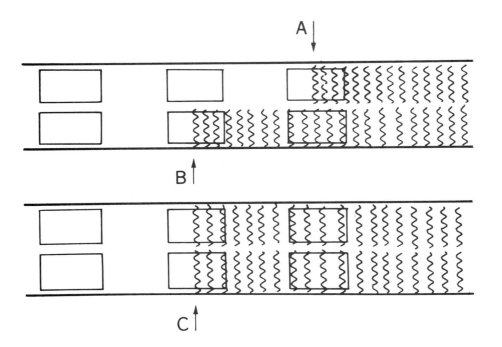

SELECTIVE SYNCHRONIZATION

In this drawing we see the three sets of heads (erase, record and play) of a standard professional half-track stereo recorder. Arrow "A" is pointing to the playback heads (one above the other). Arrow "B" is pointing to the recording heads. The wavy lines represent recorded sound.

If we have just recorded a singer (on the top track), and now want to record the same person singing in harmony with herself (on the bottom track), the singer will have to be able to listen to the track she has just recorded while *she is recording the new track.*

In a machine without sync, it would be the play-

back head picking up the old track so that she can listen, but the recording head laying down the new track. Thus the two tracks would not be synchronous, since when both are played back, everything recorded on the bottom track would be heard slightly after the top track.

But a tape recorder *with* sync will play back the top (earlier-recorded) track through what is normally its recording head. This way, each word the singer sings onto the bottom track occupies the same horizontal space on the tape (C) as its top track partner. This process is called "overdubbing."

off the *recording* head, rather than off the playback head, *while we are recording.* When the meter-and-output switch is placed in this "SYNC" position, we can monitor a *previously*-recorded track on a tape while *simultaneously recording a second track* which will be in perfect synchronization with the first.

In three-head tape recorders *without* sync, we can only listen to a previously-recorded track off the playback head, which we have seen comes a short distance after the recording head in the tape path. We could not record a second track in sync with the first on these machines because of the delay this distance causes.

For example, we record a vocalist singing a song on one track. If we then want to record her singing harmony with herself, we switch the meter-and-output switch of that previously recorded track into "SYNC," so that when the tape is played back, the first track will be picked up and reproduced at the recording head, rather than at the reproduce head as usual.

We then play the existing track through headphones so that she can hear it while she sings, and her harmony is recorded on *another track of the same tape.* This is called *overdubbing,* and is common in professional music recording. It is also very helpful in adding sound effects or music to existing recordings. "Sync" is not available on all tape recorders, but it is well worth the additional expense if it can be afforded.

CARTRIDGE (CART) TAPE MACHINES

Audio cartridge tape machines are found almost everywhere in broadcasting and in lots of non-broadcast studios too. *Carts* are used to record and play back relatively short program items (announcements, commercials, sound effects, theme music, etc.) which have to be used fairly often. A cart is a loop of quarter-inch tape on a single spindle inside a plastic case. When a cart is placed in a cart machine, the loop of tape is drawn across the heads.

A CART MACHINE
A front view of a mono ITC cart machine.

The particular characteristic that makes the cart machine useful is its ability to cue itself. *Cuing* is the process of finding a specific place on a tape or record so that it can be started by the operator precisely at that point.

When a cart recording machine is put in the "recording" mode and the transport is put in motion, a cue tone is automatically recorded at that point on the tape. When the loop of tape has come full-circle, the tape machine detects the tone and stops the transport, thus recuing the cart.

The cue tone is recorded on a separate "cue track" which is not sent to the cart machine's output, and so is inaudible to the listener.

Cart tapes come in many lengths, from a few seconds to thirty minutes. To record a two-minute public service announcement on a cart, you'll need a cart which is at least a few seconds longer than two minutes.

Carts should be "reloaded" with new tape from time to time, since the magnetic particles on the tape will begin to wear off after a hundred or so playings. Specially-lubricated tape is best because of the number of times most carts are played. Carts must be "bulk erased" because cart machines do not have the ability to erase.

Digital "carts," which consist of computer chips and require no tape at all, are beginning to replace actual carts as we have known them.

MARANTZ PMD 430 CASSETTE RECORDER

Marantz PMD 430 Stereo Analog Cassette Recorder Features three heads, for monitoring playback during recording, and either Dolby® "B" OR DBX® noise reduction.

CASSETTE TAPE MACHINES

Cassette machines operate in much the same way as reel-to-reel machines. The tape is enclosed in a container (*cassette*) with the ends of the tape permanently attached to the "reels," inside the cassette.

Most cassette machines operate at 1-⅞ ips. Most newer machines have bias and EQ (equalization) switches which allow for the use of *chromium dioxide* (CrO_2) tape.

Some cassette machines are available with three heads; many have only two. In the latter case, the right-hand head functions as both the recording and playback head. You could say that "three heads are better than two," because not only is recording quality compromised in two-head machine, but you are also unable to monitor the playback head during recording.

The better cassette machines have a meter for each channel. Cheaper models have a simpler, less accurate recording level indicator, or no meter at all. Many portable cassette recorders contain built-in condenser mics, but better results are always obtained by using a separate, high-quality microphone which is plugged into the machine via a cable.

The greatest advantages of cassette recorders are their portability and their ease of operation. One disadvantage of cassette machines is that they are less durable than their high-quality reel-to-reel counterparts. Another major disadvantage is that cassettes invariably have to be *dubbed* (copied) to open-reel format in order to be edited.

In addition, cassette recordings are generally of lower fidelity than high-quality reel-to-reel recordings, due to their slower speed, narrower tape, and less precise tape-to-head alignment. Nonetheless, advances in head design and tape formulations have brought cassette fidelity closer and closer to open-reel standards.

When shopping for a portable cassette recorder, here are some features which are important for production work: a meter; a standard ¼-inch headphone jack; a manually-adjustable recording level as well as an Automatic Gain Control; and line level inputs and outputs. Also helpful are a separate (third) head for playback and a variable speed control.

On the other hand, features which will drive up the price of a machine without adding anything useful include: big internal speakers; built-in radios; a slower speed of 15/16 ips; and all the techno-gloss packaging (fancy chrome

SONY TCD D-10 PORTABLE DIGITAL RECORDER (RDAT)

Sony TCD D-10 Stereo RDAT Recorder. A portable, digital audio recorder.

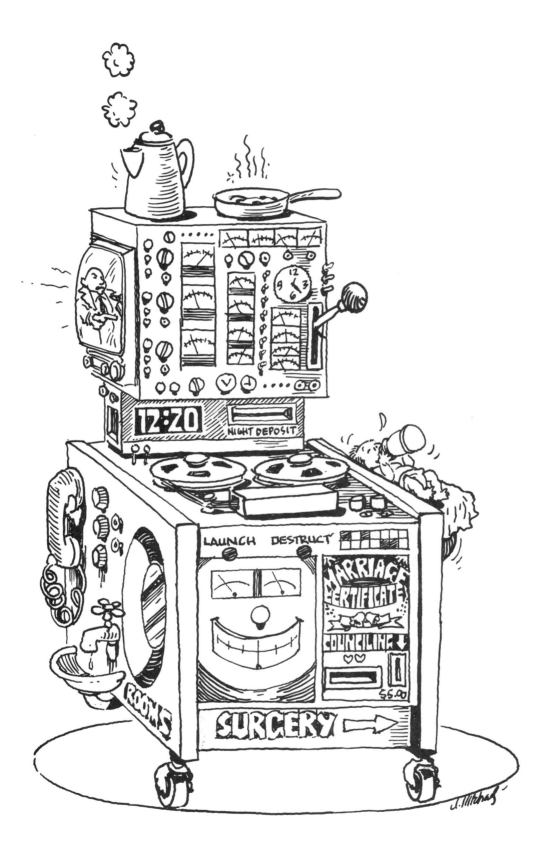

OFF-BRAND RECORDER WITH TECHNO-GLOSS PACKAGING

trim, unnecessary buttons and knobs) used to lure unknowledgeable consumers. Avoid "off-brands" that may seem like bargains, but are poorly constructed and difficult to service. Most importantly, don't be afraid to ask your friendly qualified technician for advice!

Used correctly with a good mic and good tape, modern cassette recorders can easily produce broadcast-quality tapes. Here are some guidelines for cassette recording:

- Use the machine's AC power cord whenever possible. Batteries may run down while you are recording. If batteries are necessary, *nickel cadmium* (NiCad) batteries are the best, if you have a special charger. *Alkaline* batteries last longer than cheap batteries, and are worth the extra cost.

  When you use batteries, be sure they're new or fully-charged. Weak batteries can cause the machine to run too slowly, which means your recording could sound like Alvin and the Chipmunks when played back on a machine operating at the correct speed. (Some cassette recorders have a variable speed control that can help salvage tapes where this has occurred.)

- The quality of cassette used is crucial to good cassette recording. Not only do cheap cassettes contain low quality tape, but their design and construction are often so poor as to lead to imprecise head alignment, and jamming and snarling of the tape inside the machine.

- Do *not* use anything longer than a ninety-minute cassette. The longer cassettes use very thin tape which is more likely to stretch, jam or snarl.

- Since even the highest quality cassette tape can break or become snarled in the machine, try to use cassettes whose casings are put together with screws. This type of casing can be taken apart to make tape repairs.

- Remember that the first few inches of cassette tape (five seconds are so) have no oxide coating and thus won't record anything.

- Audio cassette tapes have two small "tabs" on the "back" of the casing. These tabs engage a lever in the machine which deactivates the Record Lock built into most machines and allows the machine to operate in the record mode.

  By removing these two tabs from a cassette, you can prevent the Record Lock lever from engaging, and thus make it impossible to operate the machine in the record mode while that cassette is in it. This useful feature allows you to protect important cassette recordings from accidental erasure should someone try to re-use your cassette to make a new recording.

- Avoid using the cheesy mics which often come with, or are built into, cheap portable recorders. A professional microphone with a properly wired cable will provide the best results.

- Always make a test recording, using all the equipment you plan to use, *before* leaving home base.

- Always use earphones when recording (plugged into the recorder's monitor jack) so that you can hear any technical problems before it's too late.

- The first and last few inches of a cassette often do not maintain good contact with the heads in the machine, so it is best not to use them.

ANALOG CASSETTE/RDAT CASSETTE

The RDAT cassette, on top, is about one half the physical size of a conventional analog cassette, but the RDAT cassette is capable of holding up to two hours of information. (A 60 minute RDAT cassette is pictured.)

We've learned that inputs and outputs have three main electrical characteristics: level, impedance, and whether they are balanced or unbalanced.

TAPE MACHINE INPUTS AND OUTPUTS

LEVELS

There are three levels of inputs and outputs: mic level, line level, and speaker level. Tape machines can have mic and/or line level inputs, and line and/or speaker level outputs. Tape machines that have mic level inputs are equipped with an internal pre-amplifier. Some tape machines, including most modern open-reel studio decks, have only line inputs, and a microphone must be pre-amplified *before* being plugged into the line input of the tape machine.

MONITOR IN PLAYBACK!

Whenever possible, monitor the "PLAYBACK" ("REPRODUCE") signal while recording, instead of the "INPUT" ("SOURCE") signal. Remember that with the meter-and-output switch in the "PLAYBACK" position you will hear the actual signal that has been put on the tape, so that you will be aware of any technical problems, such as dropout, improperly threaded tape, or electronic problems *as they occur*, rather than later (when it may be too late.)

Because the recording head is often located several inches before the play-back head in the tape path, the signal you hear in "PLAYBACK" will be "delayed" for a fraction of a second. For this reason, you should be careful that the people speaking into the mics are not listening to the "PLAYBACK" signal, because it is nearly impossible for most people to speak while listening to one's own voice delayed. Instead, try it for a laugh sometime.

During recording, the technician should occasionally switch back and forth between the "INPUT" and "REPRODUCE" positions. If the "REPRODUCE" signal sounds significantly different from the "INPUT" signal, something is wrong.

Good recording technicians *always* watch the meter and *always* listen to the signal being recorded! They avoid conversation when the mics are "live" and the tape is rolling; if they are really astute, they don't even allow anyone else to make sounds of any kind during recording except those being recorded. This is absolutely necessary in order to make good recordings *the first time*. Recording is a complex craft that requires total concentration.

TOTAL CONCENTRATION

Good recording is a complex craft that requires total concentration. This person is a lot more likely to end up with a technically good program than someone who doesn't pay attention!

THE BULK ERASER (DEGAUSSER)

A *bulk eraser*, or *degausser*, is essentially an electromagnet which is strong enough to erase an entire reel of tape in seconds. It is named after Karl Friedrich Gauss, who gave his name for science.

It is standard procedure to bulk erase all tape before it is used unless it is brand new. Even though most tape machines have erase heads, small "glitches" of unerased sound may escape the erase head in the process of starting and stopping the machine. Further, a good bulk eraser will provide a more complete erasure than the erase head on a tape machine. This is particularly true if the track configuration of the tape machine on which you are erasing a tape is different from the track configuration of the machine on which it was recorded.

Here is the one and only way to do it right:

- With the reel of tape to be erased at least an arm's length away from the bulk eraser, turn the bulk eraser on. (Turning the bulk eraser on when the tape is closer than that can produce a "click" on the tape.) The bulk eraser must stay on continuously until the end of the last step.

- Bring the reel to the surface of the eraser and slowly turn the reel around and around while it is lying flat on the surface of the bulk eraser, about one rotation every two seconds.

- After at least three complete rotations, flip the reel over and rotate it at least three more times. (It may not be necessary to turn the reel over if the eraser is strong enough to erase the entire thickness of the tape.) The direction of the turning is irrelevant.

- Slowly bring the reel of tape to at least an arm's length away from the eraser. Then, and *only* then, turn the eraser off.

Cassettes and carts are erased in the same fashion. Carts in particular need to be thoroughly erased, because most cart recorders do not have erase heads. Never bring a recorded tape you want to keep along with you when you go to bulk erase another tape. Keep *all* recordings as far away from is as possible!

There are many incorrect ideas about bulk erasing, mostly because it is a skill not usually learned directly from a true master. If anyone tells you anything which seems to contradict the above rules, ask a bona fide engineer to settle the argument.

KEY TERMS TO REMEMBER

acetate
AGC
ALC
alkaline batteries
ARL
Automatic Gain Control
AUX
auxiliary
balanced input or output
bias tone
bulk eraser
calibration
cannon connector
capstan
cart
cart machine

cartridge tape machine
cassette
cassette recorder
cassette tabs
chromium dioxide
cuing
decibel scale
degausser
digital tape timer
dropout
dubbing
EIA reel
electromagnet
electronics
equalization
erase head

fast-wound
ferric oxide
ferro-chromium
flange
full-track
half-track
hiss
hub
inches per second (ips)
mechanical tape timer
meter-and-output switch
mils
monaural
mono
monophonic
multi-track tape recorder
mylar
NAB adapter
NAB reels
nickel cadmium (NiCad) batteries
open reel tape recorder
overdubbing
oxide
pack
pinch-roller
playback head

playback level control
polyester
print-through
Record Lock
recording head
recording level control
reel motors
reel-to-reel tape recorder
selective synchronization
signal-to-noise ratio
stereo
stereophonic
supply reel
sync
take-up reel
tape guides
tape timers
tensioners
three-pin connector
track configuration
tracks
transport
transport function controls
unbalanced input or output
volume unit (VU) meter
XLR connector

AUDIO CONSOLES (MIXING BOARDS)

T he main function of an *audio console* (*mixing board*) is to receive and mix together the signals from two or more audio devices (microphones, tape machines, disc players, etc.) so that the composite signal can be sent to a tape recorder, speaker system, and/or broadcast transmitter. There are boards particularly suited for broadcast situations and others more suited for recording situations, although in recent years the differences between broadcast and recording consoles have become fewer.

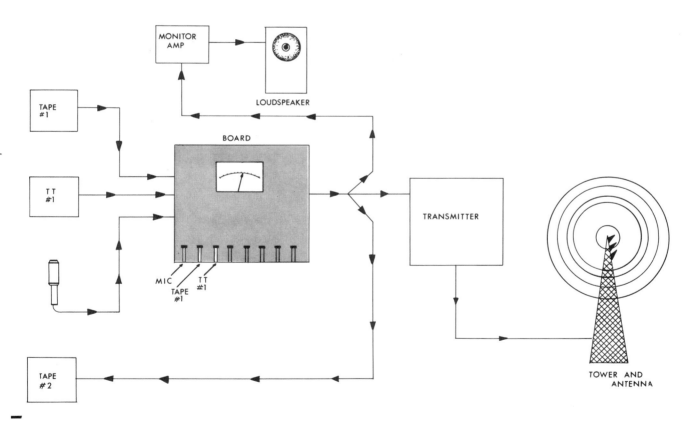

BASIC SIGNAL FLOW CHART

The outputs of several devices (tape machine, turntable 1, and a microphone) are sent into the inputs of a mixing board. Their relative volumes can be controlled there and their signals mixed together.

From the output of the board, this mix (signal) is being sent to three places:

■ A monitor amplifier and speaker, so that the mix can be heard
■ A radio transmitter, so that it can be broadcast
■ Another tape recorder, so that it can be recorded.

Recording boards contain more *processing* devices for each input signal and more potential routes through which to send the signal, and so are usually more complex. Most of the programs sent through broadcast boards (e.g. discs and pre-recorded tapes) have already been processed, so that broadcast boards don't need all of the processing gizmos required in recording boards.

A basic board contains:

■ Several inputs

■ A separate gain (volume) control for each input

■ At least one output, which is assignable to a tape recorder, transmitter and/ or public address system

■ A switch for each input which allows it to be assigned to, or cut off from, the main output channel

■ A master volume control which regulates the sum of the input volumes simultaneously (i.e., the output)

■ A means of listening to the overall mix.

Most boards also contain:

■ A meter for visual monitoring of the overall mix

■ A means of hearing each of the inputs individually for cuing.

■ An equalizer of some kind associated with each input channel.

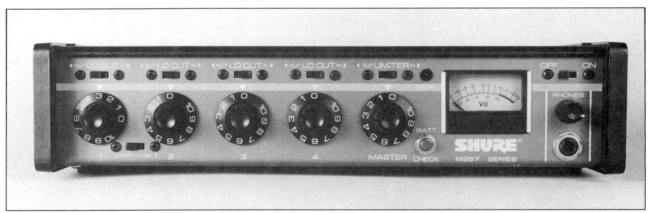

SHURE M 267 PORTABLE MIXING BOARD

This portable mixing board has four inputs (numbered in the photo above), each switchable to be mic or line level, and a single output which is also switchable to be either level.

BOARD INPUTS

Devices which are plugged into board inputs produce electrical signals which are either mic level (often called *low level*) or line level (often called *high level*). Low level inputs are used almost exclusively for microphones. High level inputs accept signals from tape machines, phonograph pre-amps, telephone or satellite connections, compressors, limiters, equalizers, tuners, noise reduction units, and the like.

The difference between mic and line level is that mic level signals must be pre-amplified so that they are brought up to line level for mixing purposes.

Microphone level inputs in mixing consoles lead first to pre-amplifiers within the consoles. For this reason, mixing boards have both mic inputs and line inputs.

Some boards contain completely separate input channels for mic level and line level signals, whereas input channels on others can be switched so as to be *either* mic or line level. Some modern recording console inputs are variable in steps all the way from mic level through line level. These controls determine how much the pre-amp for each input channel will amplify any signal sent to that input.

Both the impedance of console inputs, and whether they are balanced or unbalanced, are variable. If there is any question about these variables when connecting devices to a board, check with a technician.

BOARD OUTPUTS

Most professional mixing boards have at least two sets of outputs, which are usually balanced and line level. The output being sent to the broadcast transmitter and/or the tape recorder(s) is called the "*program*" or "MAIN" output, and is monitored by VU meters on the console. A second output, which can also be monitored by VU meters on the console, can be sent to other devices as needed. On a typical broadcast board, this second output is called the "*audition*" output.

Each input on the broadcasting console can be assigned to (sent to) either the program or audition outputs. A switch above each input volume control makes this selection.

Besides program and audition, a third kind of output that most broadcast consoles have is the "*cuing*" output. This "internal" output leads to an amplifier and speaker (usually built into the console itself), and its only purpose is to allow for listening to incoming signals without sending them to the "main" or "audition" outputs. The audition output can also be used for cuing if it is not being used for something else, but the console's cue system is usually easier to operate.

MONO, STEREO & MULTI-CHANNEL BOARDS

Each output of a *mono* board is mono, i.e., it consists of only one channel. Regardless of how many *input* channels are mixed together, the resulting *output* will be one channel—mono!

Stereo systems have two channels. Hence, the main output of a *stereo* board must consist of two separate channels. The individual *inputs* may be assigned to one or the other of the output channels (left, right, or both). The resulting output will be two channels, each carrying a different signal—stereo!

If we were to send an input signal to both output channels simultaneously at the same volume, the resulting output would be mono because both channels would be carrying identical sound information. The knob that determines to which output channel an input signal is sent is called a *pan pot*. It is called this because it can be used to move the sound from left to right and back again, as a movie camera would pan from left to right.

To accomplish a stereo mix, we need to bring together at least two input signals simultaneously, one mixed more loudly on the left output channel, and the other more loudly on the right output channel.

Some stereo boards require a separate input control for each input signal. A stereo half-track tape machine, for instance, has two outputs and would require two separate input controls in this type of console. Often the volume pots of these two controls can be yoked or *ganged* together so that they can be operated as if they were a single input. Other stereo boards combine both input signals into one input control so that each "pair" of channels is controlled by one pot as the stereo input.

MIXING CONSOLES FOR RECORDING STUDIO AND SOUND REINFORCEMENT (PA)

Most recording studio boards and public address boards are very similar in terms of their basic functions, but vary quite a lot in nomenclature and signal routing.

The board chosen to illustrate this category is made by Sound Workshop, and is a typical mid-priced, fairly sophisticated mixing console.

RECORDING STUDIO CONSOLE
The area at the right-hand end of the console is a patch panel. This is a Sound Workshop Model 34C.

This sort of console scares people half to death when they first contemplate operating it because of the enormous number of knobs, switches, and volume controls. Once you play around with it, though, you soon learn that it really only does six or eight basic things. Since it needs to be able to do those basic things to lots of different sound sources over a short period of time, like the duration of a pop tune or a reel of a movie, it is most convenient to have the basic functions duplicated sixteen, or twenty-four, or ninety times. It is very rare for someone operating a mixing console to be actively doing things to more than a dozen channels at any one time.

SIGNAL MODULE

A signal (sound) going through this module can be sent to any one, or all, of the console's "multi-track" outputs by pushing the buttons and adjusting the "panning" knob. They are called "multi-track" outputs because they are most often fed into the 24 respective tracks of a recorder. If the button adjacent to the numbers 1 and 2 is pushed, then the signal will be routed to either the console's #1 output, its #2 output, or both. If the panning knob is turned all the way counter clockwise, towards "odd," the signal will go only to the #1 output. Turning the knob all the way to "even" will send the signal only to the #2 output. If the panning knob is adjusted to a position halfway between odd and even, the signal will be equally divided between #1 and #2.

The meter on this module registers the level of signal coming into the module, rather than the module's output. Despite the fact that the meter is comprised of lights rather than a needle, it happens to be a VU meter.

INPUT CONTROL MODULE

The top left button in this section is labeled "pad." By pushing it into the "down" position you insert 20 decibels of attenuation at the module's input. This can help avoid distortion which could result from extremely loud signals overloading the circuitry in the module.

The middle button has beside it a circle with a line through it. This is commonly called a "phase reverse" switch. If the signal coming into this module is out of phase with signals coming into one or more of the other modules, the problem may be rectified by using this switch, which will change the phase 180 degrees.

The switch labeled +48 allows you to send 48 volts of "phantom" power to a condenser mic plugged into the module.

The button labeled mic/line determines whether this module is set up to receive signals from a mic level source or a line level source.

The knob in this section determines how much pre-amplification a mic will receive from this module.

EQUALIZATION MODULE

This is the equalization section of the module. The numbers around the knobs refer to the frequency to be boosted or attenuated. Each knob is actually separated into two distinct controls. The bottom half of the knob selects the frequency, and the top half determines how much boost or attenuation happens at the selected frequency.

The "low cut" button allows for the attenuation of all frequencies below a prescribed point; in the case of this console that point is 40 Hertz.

The "EQ IN" button determines whether the equalization section of the module is in the circuit, or is bypassed by signals travelling through the module.

The "MON" button determines whether the EQ section affects the "monitor" outputs or the "multitrack" outputs of the module.

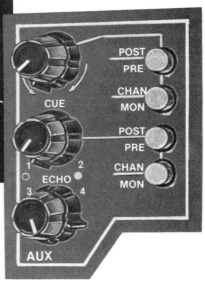

SENDS OR AUX OUTPUTS

This section of the module is usually called "sends" or "aux" outputs. The buttons and knobs allow a signal to be sent somewhere, most often outside the board, for processing. A common use of aux sends is in adding reverberation to a signal. Let's say a dry (no reverb) recording of a vocal is coming into this module. By turning the knob labeled "ECHO 1" clockwise from its present position I will be sending that vocal to the ECHO 1 output, which, by use of the studio's patch panel, can be plugged into a reverb device. The output of that device can then be sent back to the board, and plugged into a different mod-

ule, allowing the level of the reverb in the mix to be controlled.

The "POST" and "PRE" designations refer to whether the send in question comes after or before the principal volume control (fader) in the module. Sometimes it is not desirable for the level of the "send" to be affected by movements of the principal fader. In that case, the PRE/POST switch should be set in the PRE position.

"CHAN" and "MON" refer to whether the send is fed by the channel or the monitor path in the module.

MONITORING THE OUTPUT

One of the reasons that a recording studio type console like this one is more complicated than a broadcast console is that this kind of console is often used for two purposes simultaneously. When you are recording music or other material using lots of microphones, each being sent to its own track of a multi-track recorder, it is also necessary to listen to (monitor) the outputs of those mics in the control room speakers.

Sometimes you will not want to listen to the mics themselves, but rather to the outputs of the recorder tracks to which those mics have been assigned.

To perform these two basic functions we need:

1. a volume control which regulates the level of signal going from the mic to the recorder

2. a volume control which regulates the level of signal going from the relevant track on the recorder (or from the mic) into the speakers

3. a way of determining which track(s) the mic will be sent to

4. a way of determining which speaker (typically left, right, or some of both) that track or that mic will be heard through.

Much of this signal routing is controlled in the "E" section of this console. "BUS" refers to the multitrack output "bus" with which this particular module is normally associated. "TAPE" refers to the input of this module normally fed by a particular recorder track output. "MON" refers generally to the mode of operation in which the outputs of mics are being recorded and monitored simultaneously through the console. "MXDN" refers to the mode of operation in which the outputs of a multi-track tape are being mixed down (usually to a two track, left-right, mix).

The knob in the lower right of the "E" section is the "panner," which most often is used to direct a signal to the appropriate speaker and/or the appropriate track of a two track mix.

The knob on the upper left, labeled "level," is most often used to adjust the monitor level for a particular track of a multi-track recorder (during recording).

The bottom switch simply turns the module on and off.

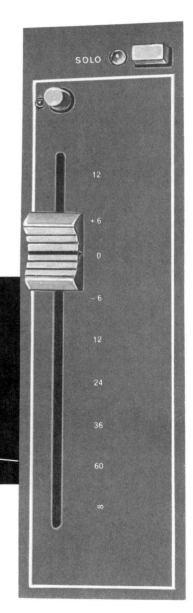

SOLO SWITCH AND FADER

The "SOLO" switch allows a signal going through this module to be sent, without interrupting its normal routing, to a separate console output bus called the "Solo" bus. This output can be made to replace what would normally be in the principal speakers so that only those signals being sent to the solo bus will be heard. The solo function can vary significantly from console to console. Read your console's instruction manual to be sure of its operation.

The "principal" fader (volume control) is the most often used part of the module. It most commonly determines the level of signal being sent to a recorder track from a mic, or from a previously recorded track to a two track mixdown.

The scale of numbers by the fader goes from +12 decibels to infinite attenuation at the bottom of the scale. The oldest joke about teaching someone how to use a fader is to say "Up is louder." And that is essentially true. Notice that you have much finer control in the area between -12 dB and +12 dB. Near the bottom of the scale even a slight movement of the fader can result in a large change in level. So, rather than try to make a fine adjustment in level with the fader in the -60 dB area, it would be advisable to find a way to raise the level of signal coming into the module by 40 or 50 dB.

Most often, and especially with automated consoles, the operator is only actively working with one, two, or three channels at once. An automated (computer controlled) console is one in which the movements of the principal faders, and sometimes other functions, are memorized by a computer. Those moves and/or switch positions can be "played back" by the computer, exactly duplicating the operator's settings. Console automation is most useful when a small number of operators, like for instance one, need to make adjustments to many different signal sources which occur either simultaneously or nearly so. She or he can do an extremely complex crossfade involving twenty faders in four seconds, one fader at a time. Only when the mix sounds right is the audio actually recorded. Until then it is only "data" that is being changed.

A typical recording studio console consists mainly of many long, narrow "modules" (some called "slices") each of which contains the faders (volume controls), equalizers, switches, etc. which allow a microphone to be pre-amplified, processed, sent to a multi-track tape recorder, and monitored through a set of speakers. There will also be several "master" volume controls which allow groups of faders to be raised or lowered by moving only one control. The console is also used to finally mix the eight, or sixteen, or twenty-four tracks which have been recorded, down to the two tracks which will be used to make the version of the project which will be heard by the public.

MULTI-TRACK OUTPUTS AND MONITOR OUTPUTS

Multi-track consoles are used most often to pre-amplify and process signals coming from microphones, then to send those signals, unmixed, to a multi-track recorder.

While this recording is happening, it is necessary to listen to the outputs of all of the relevant tracks on the recorder. Since there are not 24 separate speakers in the control room, it is necessary to mix the outputs of the recorder into the two (usually) speakers which do exist in the room.

Recording-studio type consoles of this type are set up to do two things:

■ provide a path (usually called the *channel path* from the microphones to their respective tracks on the recorder

■ provide a path (usually called the *monitor path*) from each of those tracks into the control room's principal speakers.

Eventually, a third basic function will be needed:

■ A path (usually called the *mixdown* path) by which the tracks of the multi-track recorder can be mixed and recorded onto, most commonly, two tracks (for stereo) of that same recorder or another.

KEY TERMS TO REMEMBER

audio console	low level input
audition output	mixing board
binaural mix	pan pot
cuing output	processing devices
high level output	program output

CHAPTER ELEVEN

SPEAKERS

In many ways, *speakers* (loudspeakers) are like reverse microphones. Mics generate electricity from sound, while speakers generate sound from electricity.

Most speakers operate on roughly the same principles as dynamic microphones and are called *dynamic speakers*. An alternating electrical current (the analog of our audio signal) flows from the power amp into the speaker and there through a coil of wire wrapped around a magnet. The coil of wire is attached to a thin diaphragm which is in turn attached to a large paper cone. The coil and diaphragm move back and forth at the same frequency and with the same intensity as the alternating current. This vibrates the paper cone, which vibrates the air, setting up sound waves—the reproduction of our original sound!

Electrostatic speakers operate according to the same principles as condenser microphones, through the use of a giant capacitor, and are much less common.

Different speakers, like different microphones, have different directional characteristics. Certain sizes of speaker cones reproduce certain frequencies better than others. For these reasons, there are many sizes and shapes of speakers available.

Generally, large speaker cones, called *woofers*, reproduce low (bass) frequencies best and small cones, called *tweeters*, are best for high (treble) frequencies. In addition, a middle-sized speaker cone is often used for "mid-range" frequencies.

Technically, any loudspeaker containing more than one cone is called a *speaker system*. A device called a *crossover* is used to separate the various frequency ranges in a signal and send them to the appropriate speaker cone. A speaker system which uses two sizes of cones is called *two-way*; and one that uses all three sizes is called *three-way*.

HEADPHONES

Headphones are very small speakers contained in a headset and worn against the ears. There is little difference in the frequency response between quality headphones and well-designed loudspeakers. In many instances, the choice between headphones and loudspeakers is merely a matter of preference.

However, headphones are better for listening in a noisy environment, or in a room that is of poor acoustic design (one where reflected sound will color the sound from loudspeakers). They are also very portable, and can be plugged directly into the tape machine or mixing board, without the use of a separate power amplifier.

Many folks who aren't used to headphones (for instance, people being interviewed on the radio) don't like to wear them because they feel physically uncomfortable or silly with strange devices wrapped around their heads. In this case, even though the "audio quality" might suffer somewhat if they don't wear the phones, the *overall* quality of the program will be likely to suffer much more if they are uncomfortable. On the other hand, as an audio technician, *you* should accustom yourself to wearing headphones because there are two situations in which headphones are absolutely necessary: "feedback" avoidance and "exotic" monitor feeds.

FEEDBACK

Often we are mixing mic signals in a studio which has a loudspeaker monitoring system. If the mics are turned on (*live*) while the loudspeakers are turned up, we may generate microphone *feedback*.

Feedback occurs when a signal enters the mic and is reproduced by the loudspeaker, *that* signal then enters the mic and comes out of the speaker, *that* sound enters the mic—and so on. This is called a *feedback loop*. The result ranges from an undesirable "ring" or echoing sound to an excruciating squeal, depending on how much of the loudspeaker's sound enters the microphone. No doubt you've heard feedback in PA systems at concerts, speeches and the like. Most broadcast studios have a *muting* system which avoids feedback by switching off the loudspeakers whenever a mic is turned on.

Using headphones is the only way you can listen to your mix while the mics are live. Since they fit snugly around your ears, there is little danger that enough sound can leak out to cause feedback.

"EXOTIC" MONITOR FEEDS

Another instance in which headphones are necessary is for the use of "exotic" monitor *feeds*. Here is an example encountered every day in recording studios:

A group of musicians, each playing his or her instrument, is being recorded. The musicians need to hear all of the others, but may want to hear their *own* instruments more loudly than the others, since they need to pay the most attention to their own playing. This is accomplished by sending a special mix to each musician's headphones in which they can hear their own playing a little louder than the others'.

Another situation requiring an exotic monitor feed might arise in recording a radio drama. The director, in the control room, will need to be able to give instructions to the floor manager. The floor manager must be able to hear the "mix" of the actors, and the director's instructions at the same time. If everyone could hear the director, it might result in some interesting radio *verite*, but would also likely cause considerable confusion. So a special feed is sent to the floor manager's headphones, which enables him or her to hear *both* the actors and the director.

KEY TERMS TO REMEMBER

crossover

dynamic speakers

electrostatic speakers

feedback

feedback loop

headphones

live mic

monitor feed

muting system

speaker system

speakers

three-way speaker system

tweeters

two-way speaker system

woofers

PHONOGRAPHS & COMPACT DISCS

As this book is being written the phonograph is in the process of dying as an audio format. Many purists argue that the traditional "record player" is still unmatched in some aspects by digital devices, specifically the compact disc. But the purists are definitely in the minority, and it seems likely that by the mid-1990's the phonograph will be a museum piece.

Modern phonographs consist of two basic components: the turntable and the pickup arm (which contains the stylus, or needle, and cartridge).

PROFESSIONAL PHONOGRAPH PLAYER

The two main attributes of a professional broadcast turntable are: 1) extremely fast acceleration from zero to operating speed; and 2) the ability to man-ually turn the record counterclockwise during cuing ("back-cuing").

The *turntable* is analogous to the transport of a tape machine. The turntable platter is driven by a motor, and serves to rotate the record at a precise speed. Turntables can operate at 78 rpm, 45 rpm, 33⅓ rpm and 16 rpm. Many broadcast turntables use only 45 and 33⅓.

Modern professional turntables are distinguished from "consumer" turntables by their durability, their fast acceleration from zero to full speed, and their precise speed control. Some models have strobe light indicators which enable the operator to adjust the speed.

The *pickup arm* (*tone arm*) holds the *phono cartridge* and *stylus*. As the turntable rotates, the stylus *tracks* ("rides") in the grooves of the record, and is physically vibrated by the impressions in the grooves. The movement of the stylus causes a magnet to vibrate within a coil of wire inside the cartridge, generating a very small electrical current which is sent to the pre-amp.

Most modern pickup arms have adjustable *tracking force*—the pressure exerted downward on the stylus by the pickup arm. A counterbalance weight on the end of the pickup arm is moved backwards or forwards to set the correct "weight." Too much weight on the record is damaging both to the record's surface and the stylus. Too little weight will result in poor tracking. A small scale, called a *tracking force gauge*, is used to adjust this. You should have a qualified technician show you how to make the adjustments.

Different phono cartridges require different styli, and they should not be interchanged. In addition, special cartridges and styli are needed for 78 rpm records. Using one with the other can damage the record and/or stylus.

Most modern styli are either *spherical* or *elliptical*. Spherical styli are used for broadcast and production work because they can be *back-cued*. Back-cuing is physically moving the turntable platter counter-clockwise ("backwards"), with the turntable motor off, until the record is cued.

A clean stylus in good condition is essential to accurate sound reproduction. A damaged or dirty stylus will also harm your records. To avoid damage to the stylus, *always* use the pick-up arm lift lever to raise and lower the pick-up arm. Avoid playing badly-scratched or dirty records. And *never ever* place any additional weight (paper clips), pennies, etc.) on the pick-up arm to increase its tracking force!

Even with the best of care, a stylus will become dirty in time. If a record sounds fuzzy or distorted, check the stylus for accumulated dust and oil.

The best tool for cleaning a stylus is a special stylus brush, designed specifically for this purpose. You can also use a very fine camel-hair brush. When cleaning the stylus, brush very lightly from back to front. *Never* brush from front to back or from side to side. For very stubborn stylus dirt you can try using a drop of isopropyl alcohol or disc-cleaning fluid on the brush, but be careful never to let any alcohol contact the surface of your records.

Since the outputs of phono cartridges are very low, they have to be pre-amplified just like the microphone signals. The phono pre-amp is usually external to the phonograph unit, but close by, and is almost always purchased separately. Some mixing boards contain phono pre-amps.

CARE OF PHONOGRAPH RECORDS

- Always hold a record by the center and edge. *Never* touch the grooves.
- Always put the record in a plastic or paper sleeve to protect it from the dust inside the cardboard jacket.
- Never stack records that are not in their sleeves and jackets on top of each other.

- It is better to stand a record on its edge, leaning against something, than to lay it flat.
- Never leave records in the sun, or anywhere over 75 degrees.
- Always use the tone arm pickup lever to raise and lower the arm of a record player.
- Always clean a record immediately before playing it. Use record-cleaning fluid and a record-cleaning pad. Never use alcohol to clean a record!
- Avoid playing a record more than once every few hours. Playing the record too often will actually stretch the grooves, causing distortion that cannot be fixed.
- Make sure the weight of the tone arm is under two grams.
- Make sure the needle is clean and not bent.
- Make sure that the tone arm is "tracking" well. This means moving from side to side smoothly, not putting unnecessary lateral pressure on the grooves.

The "CD," as it is more often called, is the successor to the phonograph record. It looks like a small phonograph record, but that is about where the similarity ends.

THE COMPACT DISC

Phonograph records are analog. CD's are digital.

Because they are digital, CD's are very low noise. Each "cut" can be cued instantly, and any sequence of cuts can be programmed to be played indefinitely. Not only is the CD system itself less noisy than an analog system, but it is much less susceptible to noise which is introduced from the outside. Dirt particles can quickly muck up a phonograph record, but they have little effect on a CD.

CD's work by means of a laser beam which scans the digitally encoded information. This is a "playback only" system. It is not yet possible for the user to record his/her own material on a CD at home. That's the other similarity the CD has to its uncle, the phonograph record. Digital audio tape systems are on their way to the consumer as of this writing. They have the great advantage of allowing the user to record whatever program material she/he can get hold of, and with technical quality equal to or better than the CD.

KEY TERMS TO REMEMBER

back-cuing
compact disc
elliptical styli
laser beam
phono cartridge
pickup arm
spherical styli

stylus
tone arm
tracking
tracking force
tracking gauge
turntable

CHAPTER THIRTEEN

CABLES, PLUGS, JACKS & PATCHING

A *cable* is a strand of wire, or more often several wires running parallel to each other, insulated with plastic or cloth. Each wire inside a cable conducts electricity. An audio control room is a cable manufacturer's dream, since all of the connections that must be made between the pieces of equipment in the room are made with cables.

Since these wires are very fragile, it is important to treat all audio cables with care. Never yank on a cable when disconnecting it—always grasp the body of the connector at the end of the cable and pull gently. Cables should *never* be stepped on, nor strung in places where that is likely to happen.

Cables should be carefully and neatly coiled when not in use, and should *never* be kinked or sharply bent. Because cables are wire, they can be "trained" for easy coiling, much like a garden hose. This is *imperative* for avoiding tangles and broken cables, and makes set-up easier and faster. It's worth the time and effort it takes to train *everyone* who uses cables at your facility in the proper handling and storage of cables.

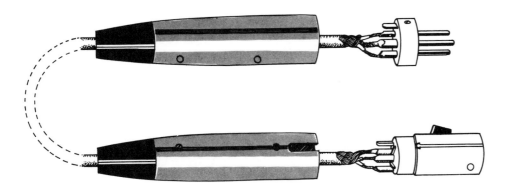

CANNON PLUG AND JACK

The "insides" of the XLR plug and jack, each at one end of a typical microphone cable. Note that there are three wires in the cable, and that each is soldered to its own metal contact at the plugs. Each of the contacts has a number by it. If the wire that is attached to pin 1 at one end of the cable is not attached to pin 1 at the other end, phase problems can result.

There are two kinds of connections between audio devices. Those which will be more or less permanent are often soldered, or *hard wired*. Other connections need to be more readily detachable, and are made with *plugs* and *jacks*. A "plug" is a connector that fits into a "jack." The jack is the receptacle, or socket, of the connection. (The plug is sometimes called the "male" connector and the jack the "female" connector.)

The five most common types of plugs and jacks you will use in audio work are:

■ XLR (*cannon*, or *3-pin*)

■ PHONE (*quarter-inch*)

■ MINI (*miniphone*)

■ TINY (*tiny-telephone*)

■ RCA (*phono*)

XLR and RCA connectors are almost always mono. Phone and miniphone connectors come in both mono and stereo forms. (Always make sure you have a stereo connector if you are sending a stereo signal through it!)

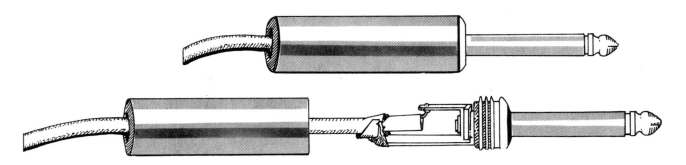

MONO ("TIP-SLEEVE") PHONE PLUG

In this mono phone plug, the "tip" is "hot"(carries the signal) while the "sleeve" is the "ground." A stereo phone plug would have a "tip," a "ring" and a "sleeve," with the "ring" carrying the additional signal.

PATCH BAYS (PATCH PANELS)

The only way to be able to interconnect all of the devices in a control room without creating a tangle of cables is the *patch bay*. A patch bay is a bank of jacks very much like an old-style telephone switchboard. Each jack is hardwired to a cable which is connected to the input or output of some piece of equipment in the room. Rather than connecting two devices together directly, we connect them by simply "throwing a patch," i.e., using a short *patch cable* or "patchcord" with a plug at each end to connect the relevant jacks at the patch bay.

If these inputs and outputs couldn't be located in one central place in the room, we would find ourselves constantly stringing cables from one piece of equipment to another.

NORMALLING

Normalling is a standard wiring procedure for patch bays in which certain outputs are "normally" connected to certain inputs. That is, there is no need to "throw a patch" from one jack to another to make a connection when the two jacks are "normalled together." This is because they are already connected by the wiring in the back of the patch bay.

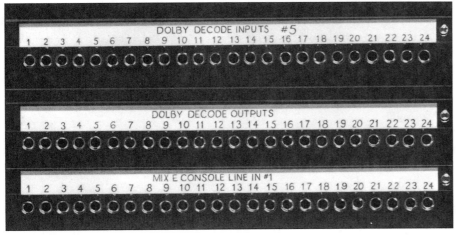

PATCH PANEL

This is a "normalled" series of patch panel connections by which a signal goes into a Dolby decoder, comes out of that decoder and goes into a mixing console input. If there were something wrong with mix console line in #6 we could avoid it by intercepting the signal with a patch cord at the #6 decode output and sending the signal into another available console input.

Patch bay connections are usually normalled between devices that frequently need to be linked together. For example, if we often need to send the output of Turntable 1 (TT1) to the input of Tape Recorder A (TR A), it is handy to have a normalled connection between the two, so that we won't have to throw a patch every time we want to connect them. Normalled connections are most common between the main output of a mixing board and the input(s) of the primary tape recorder(s) in that room.

LIFTING AND NON-LIFTING PATCH BAYS

In some patch bays, called *lifting* patch bays, if one end of a patch cord is plugged into a jack that is normalled to another jack, the normalled connection is automatically broken ("lifted"). The patch enables us to *bypass* the normalled connection and make a new connection to another jack.

For example, suppose we have a normalled connection between the output of Tape Recorder #1 (left channel) and the input of Fader #5 on our mixing console. If we plug a patch cord into the Fader #5 input jack on the patch panel then the connection from Tape Recorder #1 into that fader will be broken.

KEY TERMS TO REMEMBER

cable	patch cable (patch cord)
cannon connector	phone connector
hard wiring	phono connector
jack	plug
lifting patch bay	quarter inch connector
mini connector	RCA connector
miniphone connector	three-pin connector
non-lifting patch bay	tiny telephone connector
normalling	XLR connector
patch bay	

CHAPTER FOURTEEN
CARING FOR THE EQUIPMENT

Great audio programs of high technical quality *can* be produced using old and/or cheap equipment. The two prerequisites are good equipment maintenance and a knowledgeable operator. (By the way, the same prerequisites apply to expensive equipment.)

Just as important as learning how to use your equipment is learning to recognize the sources of problems as they occur. Further reading, expert advice, and a few years of everyday experience are the good ways to sharpen your trouble-shooting skills.

Most inexpensive equipment works according to the same principles governing the operation of expensive equipment, but is usually less durable and has slightly lower performance specifications. If you ever have a choice between buying snazzy equipment or hiring a good technician to maintain your not-so-snazzy stuff, you'd be foolish not to choose the latter.

USING CHEAP OR "CONSUMER" EQUIPMENT

You can produce good audio programs with cheap equipment *but not with poorly-maintained equipment!* Part of good production work involves knowing how to perform simple maintenance and cleaning of your equipment.

To make broadcast-quality recordings, your tape recorders must be in good shape: heads aligned, cleaned, demagnetized, and not worn out; transport operating smoothly; no intermittent connections; and recording and playback electronics working correctly. Head alignment, and transport and electronic adjustment, all should be checked regularly, but are usually best left to your maintenance technician, unless he or she has shown you how to do it yourself.

Dirty tape heads are easy enough for anyone to remedy, though, and head cleaning should become part of your everyday production routine. Tape heads always become dirty with normal use, and should be cleaned after every two to three hours of use, and no less than once a day. The importance of clean heads cannot be overemphasized. Even a barely visible film of dirt on a tape head can cause loss of high frequencies.

To clean your tape heads, use a fresh cotton swab and *denatured* alcohol. Regular isopropyl or "rubbing" alcohol will do in a pinch, but do not use it on a regular basis because it contains some impurities that can foul up the tape path themselves. Commercial "tape head cleaning solvents" are also available, but most experts agree that denatured alcohol is still the best.

Moisten the cotton swab in the alcohol, squeezing out any excess, and rub the swab briskly back and forth across the surface of the head. *Never* touch a tape head with anything metal—or anything else that might scratch its

MAINTENANCE AND CLEANING

precision-machined metal surface. Sometimes detritus from an editing pencil may get on a tape head and be difficult to remove with the swab. Use a flat, blunt wooden toothpick to remove this kind of dirt, then swab again with the alcohol.

You should also clean the rest of the tape path. This includes tape guides, rollers and tensioners, and *especially* the capstan and pinch roller. A dirty capstan and pinch roller may result in uneven tape speed.

Use cotton swabs and denatured alcohol to clean the metal parts of the tape path; the rubber components (e.g., the pinch roller) should be cleaned with a special rubber cleaning solution that is easily obtainable, as alcohol will cause the rubber to harden—which may damage the tape going across it. Again, squeeze out any excess fluid from the swab (be very careful to avoid letting alcohol drip down the capstan and into the motor bearings!). Holding the swab against the spinning capstan while the machine is turned on will allow the capstan to "clean itself."

Demagnetizing the tape heads and tape path metal components is also important for good production, because after a few hours of use these parts may build up a small magnetic charge. This is easily dissipated by using a *head degausser* (demagnetizer), which is usually shaped like a wand or small horseshoe. *Never* use a permanent magnet or any other electro-magnet, as it may be too strong a magnetic field and harm the heads.

Hold the head degausser a few feet away from the machine, and turn it on. Slowly bring it as close as possible to each tape head and each metal component in the tape path, without touching them, and then slowly move it away. Keep the degausser moving in a back-and-forth or up-and-down motion during the whole operation. This keeps the magnetic field you are generating in a totally random pattern, which completely removes any magnetic field which has built up in the heads or tape path components.

Degaussing the tape path and heads is just as important as cleaning them, and should be done before cleaning. Open reel, cassette and cart tape machines are all cleaned and demagnetized in this fashion.

When using power amplifiers and mixing boards, it's a good idea to make sure all the volume pots are turned all the way *down* before turning on the power switch. Also, make sure whatever is plugged into the power amp is switched on *before* you turn on the amp. This keeps any loud electronic "pops" from damaging components in the amplifier or loudspeakers.

When positioning or adjusting microphone stands, take care not to overtighten any of the clamps (*holdfasts*) which hold the telescoping shaft or boom in place. Overtightening this clamp can damage the threads. When using a boom stand, use the counter-weight on the end of the boom to balance the weight of the mic.

Store all connectors, adaptors, cables and the like neatly. This will make production work much easier and save a lot of time in the long run.

Here are some very good reasons *not* to allow smoking, eating or drinking anywhere near audio equipment:

- Smoke accumulates on electrical connections and creates a gummy film which will foul them up.

- Crumbs of food and tobacco will fall inside the equipment.

- Ashtrays are almost inevitably spilled.
- Drinks *are* inevitably spilled, and can totally destroy electronic circuitry.
- Smoke is particularly bad for microphones and tape heads.
- Eating and smoking leave a film on your hands which is bad for all audio equipment. (Always wash your hands before using audio equipment.)

KEY TERMS TO REMEMBER

denatured alcohol   holdfasts
head degausser

SECONDARY AUDIO DEVICES

This section covers a number of devices which will not be needed for every project, but are used when further processing of your audio signal is desired. These secondary audio devices can significantly enhance recordings within their limited capabilities. The following chapters will explain each device's advantages and disadvantages.

CHAPTER FIFTEEN

COMPRESSORS, LIMITERS, AND EXPANDERS

We've said that all natural sounds vary in volume over time, and the range of volumes from softest to loudest is called "dynamic range." Many of the sound events you will record or broadcast have a very large dynamic range.

We've also said that a certain amount of noise (in the form of hiss) is unavoidably generated by electronic devices and by the medium of analog recording. If we feed a very low level signal into an audio device, then the difference between the level of our signal and the level of the undesirable noise generated by the device itself will be small. In other words, we will have a low (poor) signal-to-noise ratio.

For example, if the quietest parts of music with great dynamic range are sent into a tape recorder at too low a level, they will be obscured by the electronic noise in the tape machine and the hiss of the tape. To improve the signal-to-noise ratio, we need to send the quietest parts of music to the recorder at a much higher level; then the level of our desired signal will be much louder in proportion to the unwanted noise—i.e., a high (good) signal-to-noise ratio.

This will indeed overcome the signal-to-noise ratio problems in our quiet passages. But now our loudest segments will be at so high a level as to cause distortion.

In discussing microphone pre-amplifiers we talked about the problem of "clipping"—the overloading of electronic circuits. Remember that a given circuit can only take a certain level of electricity; any more than that amount will cause distortion of the signal. A similar problem exists with tape. The magnetic particles can only be polarized so much and no more, without a form of distortion called *saturation*, which results in a "fuzzy" sound.

The real problem is that most audio equipment just doesn't have the capacity to reproduce the entire dynamic range of many events without an unacceptable level of noise during quiet passages, distortion during loud ones, or both. This is why compressors are used.

HOW A COMPRESSOR WORKS

A *compressor* is actually a kind of automatic volume control. Instead of someone monitoring a program constantly, turning the volume up for the quiet passages and down for the loud ones, the compressor does this itself. In other words, it "compresses" the dynamic range of the sound event.

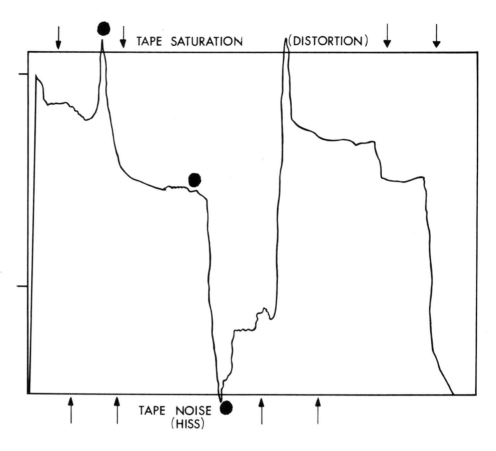

WHY WE USE A COMPRESSOR

The three big black dots in this illustration represent three different levels of loudness in a piece of music. This piece of music ranges from very quiet to very loud. The dot in the middle represents the average loudness of the piece; the top dot is one of the loudest parts; and the bottom dot is the quietest part.

During the loudest parts (the top dot), too much signal is being put on the tape for it to handle, so it will distort. During the quietest part (the bottom dot), the hiss of the tape will drown out the music.

Thus, the compromise involved in making high-quality recordings is in keeping the signal low enough so that it won't distort and loud enough so that is isn't buried in tape hiss, while trying to retain as great a dynamic range as possible.

For example: we are recording a panel discussion consisting of six panelists in a studio. The panelists will inevitably speak more loudly at some times than at others. There are also likely to be coughs, loud laughs and the like, which might cause distortion and which even the most attentive operator would not be quick enough to catch in time to reduce in level. In this situation, we plug the output of our microphone mixing console into a compressor and the output of the compressor into a tape recorder.

There are several factors which affect compression. These are:

- Threshold of compression
- Input level
- Compression ratio
- Attack time
- Release time

THRESHOLD OF COMPRESSION

The *threshold of compression* is the level of signal needed to activate the compressor. Once the signal being fed through the compressor reaches this threshold level, the compressor begins to limit the volume of the signal. The level of the threshold can usually be adjusted by turning a knob on the front panel of the compressor.

INPUT LEVEL

This is the level of signal being sent to the compressor. If *every* part of the signal sent to the compressor is above the threshold, then the dynamic range will be severely limited; every portion of the program will be at the same volume as every other portion! If *no* part of the signal is above the threshold, then the compressor will have no effect on the dynamic range of the signal whatsoever.

But when only *some* portions of a program are above the threshold, then only those portions will be reduced in volume, to a point comparable in loudness to the rest of the program, thus avoiding distortion. The input level to the compressor will be determined by the output level of the device which is feeding the compressor, and by the "input level control" of the compressor itself, if it has one.

COMPRESSION RATIO

The *compression ratio* is the *degree* to which the compressor will resist any increase in level past the threshold. On some compressors this is variable; on others it isn't. For example: if the compression ratio is set at four to one, then in order for the compressor to allow the output signal to increase by a factor of two, the incoming signal will have to increase by a factor of eight.

ATTACK TIME

Attack time refers to the length of time it takes the compressor to reduce the volume of a signal which has exceeded the threshold. Some compressors have an adjustable attack time, others don't. In either case, the time is very short, always less than half a second.

RELEASE TIME

Release time refers to the length of time it takes the compressor to allow its output signal to return to its pre-compression level. Release time is often a very important consideration.

For example, if we are recording a piece of music which has a large dynamic range, one very loud note will cause a significant amount of gain reduction by the compressor. If the release time is set too slow, then a very quiet note which immediately follows the loud one may be totally lost, because the compressor is still compressing. If release time is set too fast, and there is a quick succession of high level peaks, each followed by a short silence, a phenomenon called *pumping* may occur.

"Pumping" is an audible change in the level of low level signals during the quiet portions between the peaks, as the output level of the compressor rises sharply ("releases)". When the next signal peak comes, gain reduction occurs again, causing the low level signals to drop back down. It can best be described as a "whooshing" sound, and is sometimes referred to as *breathing*. Most compressors have an adjustable release time.

LIMITERS

When a compressor has a compression ratio of 10:1 or larger, it's referred to as a *limiter*. Limiters usually also have fast attack and release times.

A COMPRESSOR/LIMITER

SOME THOUGHTS ON COMPRESSION

Modern compressors/limiters can provide excellent protection against clipping and distortion (*overmodulation*) while still allowing a "natural" sound, i.e., without seriously affecting the listener's perception of dynamic range. In many instances, a compressed dynamic range is actually useful to the listener, since the listening environment is often filled with extraneous sounds (traffic noise, conversation and the like). Without some compression, the quieter parts of the program material would be quite difficult to hear without turning the volume up so high that the loud portions would be ear-piercing.

On the other hand, many broadcasters overuse compressors. It is a commonly acknowledged fact that people tuning up and down a radio dial will tend to be attracted to the louder stations. In the fierce competitiveness of commercial broadcasting, there is a constant battle to see which station can send out the strongest signal.

As a result, many stations try to fill every second of airtime with some sound, make every sound equally loud, and broadcast an air signal that is as loud as possible. All this is accomplished through an exaggerated use of compressors and limiters. Obviously, in this practice, fidelity takes a backseat to commercial motives.

Remember that whenever you use a compressor, however, there is some compromise between faithful reproduction and "listenability." Our goal is to respect *both* the event being recorded and the listener to the greatest extent possible.

EXPANDERS

An *expander* could be thought of as the "opposite" of a compressor, in that it *increases* the dynamic range rather than reducing it. Most expanders accomplish this by attenuating low level signals.

The most common expander found in studios is the "noise gate." Like the compressor, it also has a threshold control. The difference is that signals which are below the threshold of the expander will be attenuated (made even "quieter" than they are.) Expanders are used most often to reduce noise. Tape hiss, hum, and even unwanted background ambience can be reduced by adjusting the threshold of expansion so that the undesirable signal falls below it while the desirable signals are above it.

KEY TERMS TO REMEMBER

attack time

attenuation

breathing

compression ratio

compressor

expander

limiter

noise gate

overmodulation

pumping

release time

saturation

threshold of compression

threshold of expansion

CHAPTER SIXTEEN

EQUALIZERS

The compressors, limiters and expanders described in the previous chapter affect the overall *volume* of an audio signal. *Equalizers* affect the volume of selected *frequencies* within an audio signal.

Specifically, to "equalize" or *EQ* means to increase or reduce in volume some frequency or range of frequencies within a given sound or audio signal, while allowing the other frequencies in that same signal to pass unchanged.

A "normal" volume control increases or reduces the volume of *all* frequencies within a given signal at the same rate. An equalizer is a specialized type of volume control that allows us to control the volumes of separate frequencies within a signal separately. The bass and treble tone controls on home stereo equipment are simple equalizers.

We have already talked about the equalization that happens automatically inside tape recorders. The equalizers we are concerned with here are manually-controlled devices which are most often used to reduce the level of unwanted noise accompanying a desired signal, or to alter frequency content for a "special effect." They are often built into mixing consoles but can also be self-contained, separate units.

The simplest kinds of equalizers are *low-cut* and *high-cut* switches. When activated, these equalizers will completely filter out a fixed range of high or low frequencies. Another type of simple equalizer allows us to *boost* (amplify) or *roll off* (attenuate) a fixed range of high, low or midrange frequencies, and allows us to vary the amount of boost or roll-off.

Graphic equalizers allow us the same sort of control, but over wider and more specific ranges of frequencies. Unlike simple bass and treble controls, which lump together all the lows or all the highs, a graphic equalizer divides the audio spectrum into a greater number of frequency ranges, or *bands*, allowing us more precise equalization. Because the graphic equalizer has linear vertical slide controls, arranged side by side, there is a visual "graphic" display of which frequencies are being boosted or attenuated.

A *parametric equalizer* allows continuously variable control over all of the three equalization parameters: the *amount* of boost or the amount of attenuation, the *width* (sometimes call "Q") of the band (frequency range) being boosted or rolled off—e.g., a *bandwidth* of 100-300 Hz, and the center frequency of the band to be changed. On the other hand, with most *non*-parametric equalizers, you can only control the amount of boost or roll-off, and you must accept whatever bandwidth and whatever center frequencies the manufacturer has chosen.

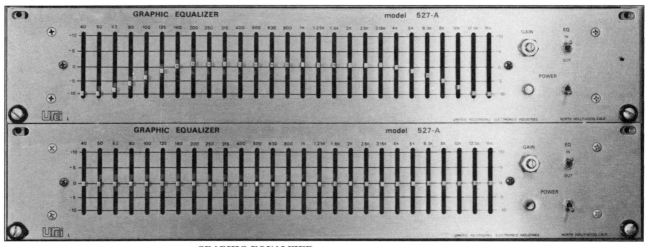

GRAPHIC EQUALIZER

A graphic equalizer allows us to control the volume of a number of the frequency ranges within a sound, and is laid out in a physical format that gives a "graphic" representation of which frequencies are being amplified and which are being attenuated.

In this photograph, the bottom equalizer is set so as to not affect the signal sent through it. The top equalizer is set to attenuate both the extreme high and extreme low frequencies. The setting would tend to reduce tape hiss at the high end and hum at the low end. But it would also substantially affect the program or sound being processed if its frequency range exceeded 100 to 5,000 Hertz.

PARAMETRIC EQUALIZER

This kind of equalizer allows the operator to determine the band (area) of frequencies to be controlled and the width of the band. Any frequency in the audio spectrum can be isolated and then either boosted or attenuated. The graphic type equalizer only allows factory determined frequencies to be controlled.

Equalizers usually have a switch which allows for all frequencies to be passed unaffected, regardless of the positions of the controls.

EQUALIZATION FOR NOISE

There are two basic kinds of *noise* encountered in audio work. *System noise* consists of unwanted signals (most often hiss or hum) which are generated by the recording system itself. *Environmental noise* encompasses such things as ventilation systems, traffic, etc. that are happening in the general location of whatever sound is the principal one to be recorded.

HISS

The *hiss* in a tape recording is noise composed of several ranges of high frequencies. We've said that there is a certain unavoidable amount of hiss always present in magnetic tape, and that hiss is generated by our audio devices themselves. (The more a device amplifies a signal, the more noise it tends to generate in the process, most of which is hiss. Microphone pre-amplifiers are traditionally the noisiest gizmos in our arsenal of electronic devices because they do the most amplification).

To equalize for hiss, begin rolling off the highest frequencies. Listen closely to the program as you do this, because as you reduce the level of the hiss, you will also be reducing the level of those same high frequencies in the program material itself.

There is a terrible compromise involved in most equalization that is done to get rid of noise. Once the noise has been mixed with the desirable sound it is very, very hard to separate the two. Therefore, for example, if the high frequencies are reduced in order to get rid of hiss there will be a simultaneous reduction of the high frequencies in the desirable sound. If the desired sound has few high frequencies then you are in luck. Unfortunately, this is not often the case.

Is it better to get rid of most or all of the noise, at the expense of those frequencies in the desired sound? Or is it better to live with more of the noise so that the desired sound doesn't have to be altered so much? This is a question that those of us who work in sound wrestle with nearly every day. Good luck!

Environmental noise presents even more complex problems in terms of the degree to which it is "treatable" by equalization. Steady state noise, like air-conditioning systems and motors are more susceptible to EQ than dynamic ones like background conversation and airplanes.

The only generalization about equalization you can rely on is the following: Most of the material you will record in your career, unless you specialize in earthquakes and tympanies, will not have much information below 60 Hertz. So the first step in "cleaning up" a noisy recording is often to reduce or get rid of everything below 60, 80, or 100 Hertz.

HUM AND BUZZ

Hum is an unwanted 60 Hertz tone caused by leakage of the AC power current into the audio circuits. Since the frequency of the alternating current electricity used to power practically everything in North America is 60 Hz, this frequency is present in very high levels in every piece of audio equipment, except those which are battery-powered.

Some of this 60 Hz signal leaks into most of the audio circuits inside every device we use, though quality audio components are designed to keep this leakage at a minimum. To complicate things further, multiples of the fundamental 60 Hz frequency are often generated simultaneously (e.g., 120 Hz tones,

240 Hz tones, etc.). When one or more of these higher frequency multiples of 60 Hz is present, the resulting complex noise is usually called *buzz*.

Some of the common sources of hum and buzz are poorly grounded equipment, improperly-connected devices, or cables with broken or faulty wiring. Solutions to hum and buzz problems are often fairly complicated, but the first thing to check is the cables. Replace them and the hum may disappear. Whatever the source of the noise, by far the best time to deal with it is *before* the recording is made. Never assume that you will be able to eliminate hum or buzz after the fact with an equalizer.

However, sooner or later in your career as an audio technician, some disappointed novice will bring you a tape he or she has produced, asking if you would please get rid of the buzz or hum which cohabits said tape with this person's lovely, scheduled-to-be-broadcast-this-afternoon program.

Equalizing for hum is done the same way as equalizing for hiss, except that the frequency being filtered is a low frequency (60 Hz). Equalization can usually reduce the level of the hum, but it can never get rid of the problem completely.

Buzz is *much* harder to filter because it is made up of several frequencies, generally multiples of 60 Hz. Attempts to filter these low and midrange frequencies will have a more noticeable effect on the program, because our hearing is more sensitive to changes in these frequency ranges than to changes in high frequencies.

THOM'S LAW NUMBER 61: Take time to record it correctly in the first place! The laws of karma will reward you in many ways.

EQUALIZATION FOR EFFECT
How Does He Make His Voice Do That?

A more creative use of equalization is the alteration of sounds for "special effects." For instance, often when we hear a radio program containing a simulated telephone conversation, one voice is being equalized to approximate the frequency response of a telephone line.

Both the microphones used in telephones, and the lines used to carry normal telephone signals, have a very narrow frequency response. They reproduce only those midrange frequencies between approximately 500 and 3,000 Hz. So in order to simulate a phone conversation, we boost only those midrange frequencies, and attenuate the highs and lows. (Note that you can reverse this equalization on recordings of *real* phone conversations to make them much more listenable!)

This "telephone effect" is one of a number of "aural illusions" that equalization can provide for radio listeners. Other illusions that can be created by equalization include dreams, "thinking aloud," flashbacks in time, robot voices, or voices coming from far away.

PUBLIC ADDRESS SYSTEM "EQ"

Another common use of equalization is to "adjust" or "tune" a PA system to the environment in which it is to be used. All acoustic environments (rooms, auditoriums, outdoor theaters, city streets, etc.) have their own unique frequency response. Each tends to accentuate certain frequencies and "swallow up" others, due to such factors as the size and shape of the place, how it is enclosed, and the number, texture and dimensions of everything within the enclosed area.

In the extreme, these tendencies can cause feedback by reflecting sound from the speakers back into the microphones. Boosting or attenuating certain ranges of frequencies in the PA system can help compensate for these tendencies, avoiding feedback and providing a more lifelike reproduction of the sound.

Many microphones contain a simple equalizer, which allows for varying degrees of bass frequency attenuation. This kind of EQ serves two purposes. One is to compensate for the tendency of directional microphones (i.e., everything but omni's) to overemphasize low frequencies when the sound source is within a few inches of it (proximity effect).

OTHER USES OF EQUALIZATION

A bass roll-off switch is also useful in preventing mechanical vibrations, like those caused by someone walking across the floor, from being reproduced by the microphone. Since these vibrations are usually very low in frequency, rolling of all frequencies below 50 or 100 Hz will reduce these unwanted signals.

In summary: since the perception of sound is subjective, there are no hard and fast rules governing when or how much equalization is appropriate for any situation. The best way to learn how to use equalizers well is to experiment with them.

KEY TERMS TO REMEMBER

attenuate	high-cut switch
bandwidth	hiss
boost	hum
buzz	low-cut switch
environmental noise	noise
EQ	parametric equalizer
equalization	roll-off
graphic equalizer	system noise

CHAPTER SEVENTEEN

NOISE REDUCTION DEVICES

Noise reduction devices are electronic systems which use compression, equalization and expansion to *avoid* some of the noise inherent in audio tape and circuitry. They do *not* "cure" or get rid of noise which is *already present* in recordings. Rather, noise reduction devices are used as part of the recording process, in order to avoid the noise inherent in that process.

The most common systems used today are *Dolby®* and *DBX®*.

DOLBY®

There are four main kinds of Dolby® used in audio production work. They are referred to as "A," "SR," "B," and "C". Type A is the system used in most professional applications, though it may be overcome in the next few years by SR. Type B is still the most common in "non-professional" systems, though it is losing ground to C.

Eventually they will all be made unnecessary by some version of digital recording, though not in the next year or two.

DOLBY® MODEL 363 NOISE REDUCTION UNIT

This two channel device can provide either "A" or "SR" type noise reduction, depending on the position of the switch at the lower right. In SR mode this unit can give an analog two track recorder approximately the same signal-to-noise performance as a digital recorder.

The left-hand SR/A card is shown only partially inserted.

Dolby®, like all noise reduction systems, is a two-part process. An audio signal is fed into the Dolby® unit, where it is *encoded* before being sent to the recording head of your tape recorder. The encoding process involves boosting certain bands of frequencies during the *quiet* portions of the program, so that they will be closer in level to the same frequencies in the louder portions.

When the program is played back, the signal from the playback head must be sent through the Dolby® unit to be *decoded*. (The same device is used both for encoding and decoding.) In decoding, those bands of frequencies which were previously boosted during encoding are attenuated by exactly the same amount, and again *only* during the quiet portions of the program. The effect is to restore the original relationship between all the frequencies in the quiet parts and the loud parts of the program.

The tape hiss and other noise generated during recording (*after* encoding and *before* decoding) was *not* boosted, but *will* be attenuated. Thus it will be much lower in level in relation to the desired signal—in other words, we have achieved a better signal-to-noise ratio.

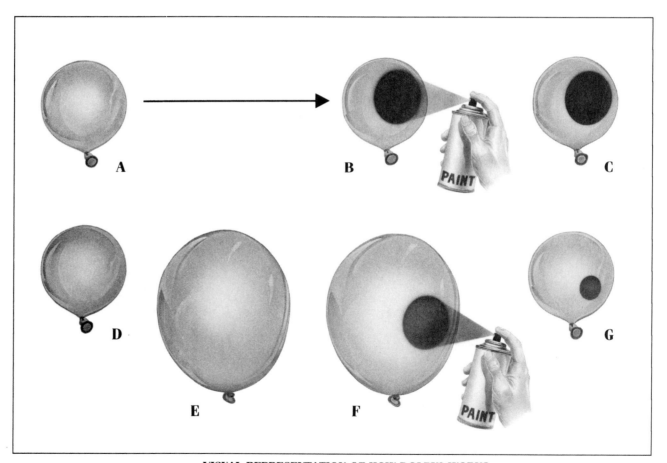

VISUAL REPRESENTATION OF HOW DOLBY® WORKS

In this analogy the balloon represents a sound. The spray paint represents the noise which will be added to my sound when I store it, for instance, on tape. When I play back my sound from the tape it will carry with it a certain amount of noise, balloon "C." If, on the other hand, I blow up the balloon before it gets sprayed, "E," when it's reduced to normal size the amount of noise will be significantly less, "G." The blowing-up of the balloon beyond its normal size is analogous to the Dolby® encoding process. Reducing the balloon back to its normal size is analogous to the Dolby® decoding process.

"B" and "C" only deal with high frequency noise, so they are mainly for tape hiss. "A" and "SR" reduce noise in several bands of frequencies so are helpful with mid and low frequency noises in addition to highs.

A Dolby® "A" or "SR" unit will have:

■ A meter

■ A switch which selects the encode or decode mode

■ A switch which allows a signal to pass through the unit unaffected

■ A switch which sends a *Dolby tone*® to the output of the unit

DOLBY® TONE

It is standard practice to record a zero VU level tone at the beginning of all reels of tape which contain Dolby® encoded programs. This is so that the level of the signal being sent through the Dolby® unit during decoding will be identical to the level sent through the unit during encoding. During decoding, the tone should register zero VU on the meters of the tape machine *and* on the Dolby® unit VU meter.

If reproduce levels are not so calibrated, the decoding process may not be a mirror image of the encoding process. The most noticeable result of improper calibration will be either too much or too little high frequency reproduction. In other words, the reproduced signal will sound "brighter" or "duller" than it should. Dolby® tone is not usually used with "B" or "C".

DBX®

DBX® is the second most common method of noise reduction. It is similar to Dolby® in that it compresses the signal during recording, and expands it during playback. However, no calibration tone is required with DBX® because compression and expansion take place at all signal levels, not only during quiet passages.

The compression ratio in the DBX® system is twice as large as it is in Dolby® "A". Theoretically, this allows for greater noise reduction capability, but practically it has two commonly-encountered drawbacks:

■ The compression and expansion are sometimes audible, resulting in a slight "breathing" sound.

■ The system is such that tape dropout and other equipment imperfections may be emphasized.

SOME NOTES ON NOISE REDUCTION

When working with noise reduction systems, remember:

■ A signal *cannot* be compressed or equalized between encoding and decoding without destroying the utility of the noise reduction processing! Any compression or equalization should be done either before encoding or after decoding.

■ The preferred way to make an encoded copy of an encoded recording is to go straight from one tape machine to another *without* decoding the tape. If a decoded copy is desired, then obviously a decoding unit must be placed between the machine which holds the original tape and the machine onto which the new recording is to be made.

KEY TERMS TO REMEMBER

DBX®	noise reduction devices
decoding	Type A Dolby®
Dolby®	Type B Dolby®
Dolby® tone	Type C Dolby®
encoding	Type SR Dolby®

CHAPTER EIGHTEEN

ARTIFICIAL REVERBERATION

When we hear a sound in a room, in a forest, or in a cave we are hearing not only the sound as it travels directly from source to ear, but also after it has bounced off many kinds of surfaces before it gets to our ears. If the acoustic space has lots of hard, smooth surfaces, like a tiled bathroom, a voice, for instance, may continue to bounce around for a considerable time after the person speaking or singing has stopped vocalizing.

As we grow up our ears become highly tuned to the various kinds of acoustic spaces. Slightly unusual spaces are often fascinating to us. Ever notice how many people can't resist blowing their car horns when driving through a tunnel?

Artificial reverberation has been used at least since the 1950's in popular music. The sound of a musical instrument could be made to cause a metal plate to vibrate. The plate would persist in vibrating for a period of time after the initial sound died away, simulating in a crude way the behavior of *natural reverberation* and *sound decay*.

In recent years digital devices have become available which can simulate real acoustic spaces with an amazing degree of accuracy. Everything from a

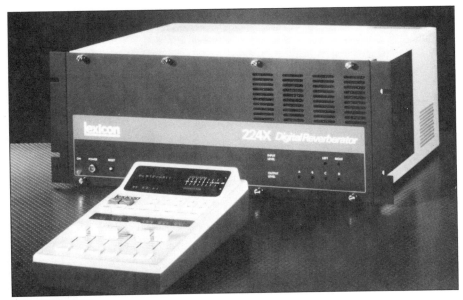

LEXICON 224X

One of the most sophisticated artificial reverberation devices is the Lexicon 224X. It can simulate many different kinds of acoustic spaces, and the user can create his or her own programs by altering such parameters as decay time and equalization.

closet to the Taj Mahal can be fairly easily duplicated. These devices are used in music to simulate concert halls and for special effects, and in film and radio drama to make actors who are recorded in a studio sound like they are actually in some "real world" acoustic space.

The best of these digital reverb devices come with pre-programmed spaces, and they also allow the user to create his or her own spaces and store them in the device's memory.

KEY TERMS TO REMEMBER

artificial reverberation   sound decay
natural reverberation

PRODUCTION!

There are three general kinds of technical operations involved in producing any type of audio program on tape:

- Using microphones to record speech, music or other sound. Recording may involve mixing several microphones (or other sound sources.)

- Editing these recordings (choosing what to keep, and in what order.)

■ Mixing these recordings—along with any other sound elements we wish to include in our final program— onto a single tape, which is our finished production.

CHAPTER NINETEEN

SETTING UP THE CONTROL ROOM

Most production is usually done in a *control room* or *production room* containing the mixing console, one or more disc players, and two or more open-reel tape recorders. It can in addition contain a number of other sound sources (cassette machines, cart machines and mics) which can also be mixed through the console, as well as other audio processing devices.

There are some general set-up procedures for the control room, that should always be observed before you go to work:

■ Clean the control room and studio. Everybody and everything will work better in a clean environment.

■ Clean the heads and tape paths of all the tape machines you will be using.

■ Bulk-erase any tape you plan to use (unless it's brand new).

■ Plug in all the mics you plan to use, and have someone speak into them. Adjust the console pots so that you get good readings on the console meters. Listen for mic and cable problems (hum, buzz, etc.).

■ Adjust the recording level controls on the tape recorder so that the tape recorder meters register the same levels as the board meters. Sending a tone through the board and into the recorder is the most accurate way to do this, but it can be done reasonably well with someone speaking into a mic. The console's master output volume should be set between 60% and 85% "open."

■ Make test recordings with all the tape machines on which you will be recording:

1. Set the "INPUT" and "PLAYBACK" volume controls at their normal positions.

2. Put the meter-and-output switch in "INPUT" position.

3. Start recording a voice or other sound. A pure tone is best. Adjust the microphone level so that it is registering zero VU on the tape recorder meters.

4. Switch the meter-and-output switch to "PLAYBACK" while watching the levels. If the meter changes by more than 2 dB, one of several things may be wrong.

   —You may have twisted the tape. Check to make sure it is threaded properly.

—The tape you are using may not be compatible with the bias setting of the machine. Try a different kind of tape.

—There may be something seriously wrong with the tape machine itself. Ask an engineer for help.

If you have a *tone generator*, the above test will be much more accurate. It will also enable you to spot dropouts in the tape you are about to use before it is too late. Also, monitor the test recording to make sure the machine is reproducing accurately.

■ Be sure all the console pots you *don't* plan to use are turned down.

KEY TERMS TO REMEMBER

control room   tone generator
production room

CHAPTER TWENTY

USING MICROPHONES

Making an original recording involves mixing the outputs of some number of microphones so that the sounds being picked up by those mics can be broadcast or recorded for later use (or both). To effectively record any original material, we must follow some basic guidelines regarding the use of microphones.

GUIDELINES FOR MICROPHONE USE

- Find out what the "pickup pattern" of your mic is—i.e., that area for which your microphone is designed to have the best response. A mispointed microphone will result in a poor recording.

- Correct microphone *placement* is even more important in miking than the *type* of microphone used.

- The farther a mic is from a sound source, the more of the acoustic environment (ambience) it will pick up in proportion to the sound source itself.

- Unwanted effects will result from a microphone being placed too close to a sound source, particularly a human voice. They include:

  —"Popping," caused by rushes of air resulting from the pronunciation of certain consonants such as p, b, f and t.

  —Over-emphasized bass frequencies

- The intelligibility of voices tends to be better with relatively close miking.

- The optimal distance for miking a voice under normal conditions is from six to twelve inches. In "on-the-street" interview situations, where there is a lot of unwanted ambient sound, three to four inches is likely to be better.

- A *windscreen* (a foam cover for a microphone) may be needed when close-miking a voice to help avoid popping. Only certain kinds of foam can be used; the wrong kind will block out most of the high frequencies.

- Too many mics in a small area may create sound problems. A good rule of thumb is that each microphone should be placed at least three times as far away from every other mic as it is from the source to which it is assigned.

- Extremely loud sounds may cause a microphone to overload its pre-amp. A "pad" may be inserted between mic and pre-amp when a variable gain pre-amp is unavailable.

- If a mic appears to be malfunctioning, try another mic cable first. The problem is more likely to be the cable than the mic.

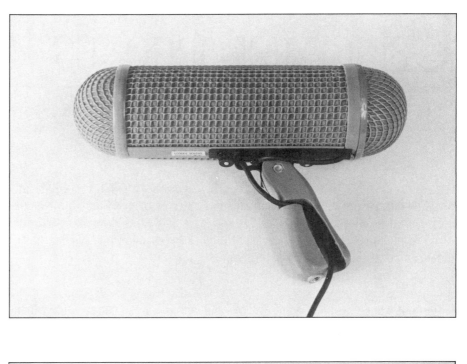

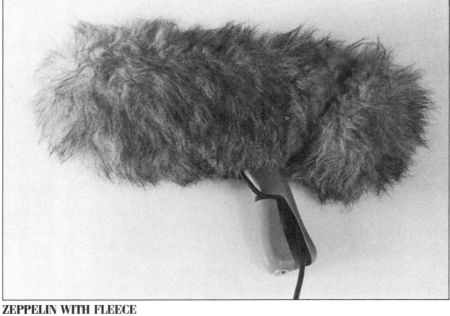

ZEPPELIN WITH FLEECE

Above, a Rycote "zeppelin" style microphone wind-screen and pistol grip. Below a Rycote Windjammer fleece wind guard mounted on a zeppelin. This degree of wind protection will result in altered directional characteristics and frequency response, but in high wind conditions the compromise may be well worth it.

- Do not *ever* blow into a microphone! When you need to check a mic, speak into it or make a noise in front of it.

- Most microphones are very sensitive to "handling noise." Anything that rubs against the mic, mic cable or mic stand can generate loud, unwanted noise.

To avoid this, keep your fingers perfectly still while holding a "live" mic, and don't let anything touch the mic, the cable or the stand.

■ Omnidirectional mics are often a better choice for on-the-street interviews than unidirectional mics. Besides making a two- or three-way conversation easier to mic, they are less sensitive to handling noise, popping, wind noise, and proximity effects. Also, they are usually more rugged, and often cheaper.

■ When recording live acoustic music, it is not always necessary to have a separate microphone assigned to every voice and every instrument. (More on this later.)

■ In voice recording, attention should be given to *sibilance*—the high frequency hissing, almost whistling sound people produce when pronouncing certain consonants such as "s," "ch," "j" and "z".

Microphones tend to exaggerate this sound, especially when placed directly in front of the mouth. We can reduce sibilance by placing the microphone above, below, or to one side of the mouth, without sacrificing frequency response—*as long as the mic is still pointed directly at the mouth*. This mic placement is also useful to avoid popping.

AMBIENT NOISE PROBLEMS

The best way to avoid picking up unwanted sounds during a recording is to place the mic(s) as close to the sound source as possible. How many potential ambient noise problems can you spot here?

■ If a recording session has to be stopped and restarted on another day, it is important to use the same microphones and the same mic placement as before.

■ In order to make a voice sound like it is coming from some distance away, it is sufficient for the person who is being miked to simply turn the head away from the mic 180 degrees.

MIC POSITION

The first position of the mic illustrated is the most commonly accepted for picking up a voice. The mic should point directly at the mouth and should be six inches to a foot away.

The second position, though, is an alternative worth trying. It has two big advantages over the first: 1) it avoids picking up too much sibilance, because high frequencies tend to travel in straight lines from the mouth; and 2) the mic will be less susceptible to "popping" if it is not directly in front of the mouth. The mic should still be pointed *at* the mouth, but from above rather than in front.

In the third position, our friend has decided to become an opera singer. Distant positioning of the mic like this will result in picking up much more of the room sounds, echo, etc., which may be undesirable.

■ Avoid making recordings in places where there is background noise from air conditioners, fans, fluorescent light hum, heaters, refrigerators, open windows, other conversations, etc. These extraneous sounds are much more easily ignored when the person speaking is visible, because the mind of the listener uses the visual aids of lip and body movements and facial expressions to help "focus" on what the speaker is saying. In a purely aural context (radio), there are no visual clues, and the listener is much more easily distracted by extraneous sounds. The ideal, therefore, is often to have what you want to record be the sole sound the listener hears. (This is not to say that environmental ambience is always undesirable—when properly used, on-location background sounds can lend warmth, presence and a touch of reality to your recording.)

PHASE

Suppose we are recording a person speaking into a microphone. The mic generates an alternating current of electricity which flows through two of the three wires of the mic cable (the wires connected to pins 2 and 3 of the cannon

NO

YES

plug). These alternating currents eventually cause a speaker cone to move in and out, generating sound.

Let's say we now put *two* mics in front of this same person, and connect the two mics to a mixing console where they will be mixed together and sent to a single output and finally to a speaker. But let's rewire one end of one of the cables so that the wire leading from pin 2 at one end now leads to pin 3 at the other end, and vice versa.

Now, when the signals get to the console, the electricity will be flowing one direction coming from one cable and the *opposite* direction coming from the other cable. When they are mixed and sent to a speaker, the signal from one cable will be trying to make the cone move out while the signal from the other cable will be trying to make the cone move in! The two signals cancel each other out.

Two such oppositely wired cables are said to be "out of *phase*" with each other. This problem happens mostly with mic cables because they have to be frequently rewired due to breakage, and miswiring is always a possibility. Phase problems, though, can result in any situation where two cables carrying identical (or nearly identical) signals are accidentally wired oppositely with respect to each other.

This problem occurs also when two microphones are positioned so that a single sound causes the element of one mic to vibrate out of phase with the element of the other. For this reason, it is a good idea to mix into one channel the outputs of all the mics in a *multi-mic* setup (*sum* the mics) one by one and listen for a drop in level or change in frequency response (tone quality) as each mic is added. If such a change occurs, you know that the last mic is significantly out of phase with at least one of the others.

If the *phase cancellation* is due to the mic's placement, changing its position in the room should solve the problem. The closer each of the mics is to its sound source, the less likely it is that this problem will occur. (The phase cancellation may also be due to a faultily-wired cable. In this case, replacing the offending cable should remedy the situation. Don't forget to have the cable rewired later!)

DISTANT (SIMPLE) MIKING

Musical performances which are not amplified (*acoustic* music) provide good opportunities to try *distant miking* techniques. A good acoustic group does their own "mixing" naturally, adjusting the volumes of their instruments and voices as they play so that one doesn't drown out another. For this kind of music, it may be best to use only one or two mics, placed so that each instrument is heard at an acceptable level.

This kind of miking requires a good acoustic environment, one with no undesired ambience (noise) or harsh reflected sound. Since we're using only one or two mics, they may not even need to go through a mixing console *if* our tape recorder has mic inputs.

Here are some suggestions:

■ Try placing the musicians around a single omnidirectional mic, or on both sides of a single bidirectional mic, with the loudest instruments farthest away from the mic.

■ Try placing a mic five to twenty feet out in front of the musicians. The natural reverberation (of a good concert hall, for instance) may make the music even prettier. If there is an audience, you can use a special, telescoping extra-tall mic stand to raise the mic above the level of the crowd noise.

- For stereo recording, cross two unidirectional mics roughly at right angles to each other, in front of the musicians. This is called a *coincident pair, crossed pair, or X/Y miking*, and will provide a good stereo mix.

Placing mics at *opposite* of the group will *not* give a true stereo sound, and may also cause phase problems.

CLOSE (MULTI-) MIKING   If the music we are recording or broadcasting is "amplified" (using electric instruments), or if the acoustic environment is poor, we'll want to place the mics within inches of the sound sources to which they are assigned. There are other good reasons for close miking as well:

- To make sure that each sound source will be picked up primarily by its own mic and sent to its own volume control, so that each volume can be controlled independently.

- To make sure that each voice or instrument will be as loud as possible in proportion to the ambient noise (e.g., crowd noise, or sound coming from PA speakers).

- To make sure that the sound from each voice or instrument will enter the mic loudly enough to minimize the amplification needed to mix and record it (the more amplification, the more electronic noise generated.)

Once you have decided on a miking scheme and have initially positioned your microphones:

1. Sum your mics (as described in the above section on "Phase").

2. Turn the volume of your headphones up higher than normal and listen very closely for hum or buzz. The most likely cause of this problem is a bad mic cable.

3. *Always* make a test recording and listen to it so that any problems can be corrected before the performance begins.

MIXING MICS TO STEREO   When recording in stereo, remember that we are essentially assigning each of our two console output channels to its own separate track on the tape recorder. When miking with the simple "crossed pair" technique, we would assign the input signal from one mic to the left channel, and the input signal from the other mic to the right channel.

When doing a *multi-mic* mix for stereo, we need to assign each input to one channel or the other, *or both*. A general rule for stereo mixing is that the main (lead) instruments are assigned to both channels (using the pan pots), which will make them sound as though they are "in the middle" of the group, when we play back the tape. Back-up instruments can be assigned primarily to one channel, but they should still be kept slightly in the other as well, for the most realistic effect. An instrument assigned to both channels will sound louder than an instrument assigned to only one channel, unless you mix the instrument on two channels at a lower level.

Always remember that many radio listeners will not be able to listen in stereo. Your mix must sound good in mono, too. Often an instrument in a mix will sound just fine in stereo, but will seem to "disappear" when heard in mono.

Because you are mixing in stereo, you will hear an "added dimension" of sound. It is easy to have one instrument in the left channel sound okay when compared to an instrument in the right channel. But when you sum the two and listen in mono, one may actually be overpowering the other. The only way to adjust for this is by monitoring your mix carefully, occasionally switching your monitor from stereo to mono.

When mixing music, remember that a good operator will allow what the musicians are doing at any given moment to determine how the music is being mixed. At times, musicians will take a "solo" and need to be featured (mixed to the "foreground"). Also, remember that good mixing involves *reducing* the level of musicians who sound too loud, as well as boosting the level of musicians who sound too low. It's easy to fall into the trap of always boosting the input faders of the musicians who sound too soft, without ever lowering the volume of the loud ones. Eventually all of the inputs will end up being set too high, and you'll have to drop the level of the master volume control to keep the overall signal from overloading whatever it is feeding.

MIXING LIVE MUSIC

KEY TERMS TO REMEMBER

acoustic miking
coincident pair
crossed pair
distant miking
multi-mic mix
phase

phase cancellation
sibilance
summing the mics
windscreen
X/Y miking

CHAPTER TWENTY–ONE

EDITING

There are two methods of editing a tape recording: *cut-and-splice* editing and *electronic* editing. Cut-and-splice editing (or simply *splice editing*) is the actual physical removal and/or rearrangement of selected pieces of the tape. Electronic editing is the selective copying (dubbing) of certain portions of the recording onto another tape.

Let's say that we have just taped in interview. There may be several reasons why you, as the producer of the piece, will want to eliminate or rearrange some of the words or ideas expressed in the interview.

■ The people interviewed may have said something that they now wish removed from the recording.

■ There may be words which FCC regulations say you cannot broadcast.

■ The ideas expressed in the interview may be more easily understood if their sequence is changed (rearranged in time).

■ The length of the interview may exceed the length of time allotted to its broadcast.

■ There may be an excessive number of pauses, stammers, mispronounced words, etc. (This is not to say that all "imperfections" in recorded dialogue should be removed, as often they are an important part of the character of the interview.)

Look at the representation on the next page of how the sentence "I hate folk music" would look if we could see it as it was being recorded on a piece of tape.

Let's say the person being interviewed actually hates *all* music and insists later that the word "folk" be removed from that sentence. The easiest way to accomplish this is to simply cut out the piece of tape which has the word "folk" on it, and then join together (*splice*) the two remaining pieces of tape so that the word "music" now follows the word "hate."

In order to make an edit like this, we need:

■ A "wax" marking pen (*china marker* or *grease pencil*) for marking the places to be cut.

■ A razor blade, for making the cuts.

■ A *splicing block*, for holding the tape while it is cut, guiding the angle of the cut and aligning the ends to be rejoined.

CUT-AND-SPLICE EDITING

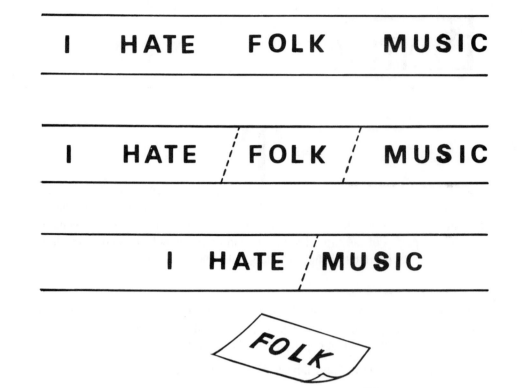

TAPE EDITING BY SPLICING

Since most tape recorders transport the tape from left to right, this is actually the way the sounds get put on the tape itself. Think about it. Most tape editing is simply a matter of physically cutting out unwanted words or phrases and joining the remaining pieces with adhesive tape.

- *Splicing tape*, for rejoining the ends of the tape.

The key to splicing is this fact: at the instant we hear a sound being reproduced by a tape machine, *that sound is directly over the center of the playback head*. This allows us to precisely locate individual sounds on a strip of tape so that we know exactly where to cut.

There are two ways to locate the place to be cut:

- By making a mark with a china marker on the backing of the tape *directly over the center of the playback head*. This method is accurate, and is easy to comprehend; but wax from the pencil can get smudged onto the surface of the head. This method demands a frequent, thorough cleaning of the tape path.

- Some people prefer not to mark the tape directly on the playback head. Also, on some machines there is no easy access to the playback head, and it is difficult or impossible to reach it with a china marker. In this case:

  1. Find and mark a convenient place, other than the playback head, somewhere along the tape path on which to mark the tape.

  2. Measure the distance from that point to the center of the playback head.

  3. On the splicing block, measure the same distance from the cutting groove and make a permanent mark there.

4. After marking the tape at your new reference point, put the tape in the splicing block, and align the mark on the tape with the mark on the block.

5. The point on the tape which is now at the cutting groove of the editing block will be the point which was at the center of the playback head when you marked the tape. This is your cutting point.

To complete the splice, butt the edges of the two pieces of recording tape together in the editing block, with the backing side up (oxide side down), and carefully place a one-half to one inch length of splicing tape over the juncture of the ends of recording tape, bonding them together. The splicing tape must not be hanging over the edges of the audio tape! The technique of getting the splicing tape exactly positioned requires some practice. Run your fingernail back and forth firmly across the splice to insure a good adhesion. There should be no air bubbles between the splicing tape and the recording tape.

Carefully remove the spliced audio tape from the lock by grasping it at each end of the block and tugging in a gentle "snapping" motion. Do not peel the tape out of the block because this will cause the tape to crinkle. Always listen to your spliced segment to make sure your edit is correct. Like most production work, skillful cut-and-splice editing requires a lot of practice. Some hints:

■ Use a new razor blade. Blades tend to become dull after a few hours' use, and a dull blade makes splicing a lot more difficult. Blades also become magnetized after prolonged use. A magnetized blade will put a magnetic signal onto the audio tape, which will result in a clicking sound at that point on the tape.

■ Use the diagonal groove on the splicing block for most splices. This makes a more durable splice and provides a better angle between the pieces of tape being spliced together, making it sound less like a splice. Use the perpendicular groove only when extremely precise cutting is required.

■ It is not necessary to bear down on the razor blade when making a cut. This just wears out the block and the blade faster.

■ It is easy to make the mistake of twisting the audio tape while making a splice. Don't splice the backing of one piece of tape to the oxide side of the other piece of tape!

■ Never throw away any piece you've edited out until you have listened to the whole segment containing the splice to see if a mistake has been made.

LEADER TAPE, HEADS AND TAILS

Leader tape is colored (or sometimes clear) plastic or paper tape which has the same dimensions as audio tape but does not have a magnetic oxide coating. It is used for several purposes:

■ As a visual cue marking the exact beginning or end of an audio program or program segment.

■ As a means of separating segments of a program which need to remain in sequence on the same reel.

■ To facilitate threading of a tape, preventing the beginning or end of a program from becoming frayed or broken.

- To denote whether a reel is wound to the beginning (*heads out*) or end (*tails out*) of a program. This is accomplished by always using one color of leader for the heads and another color for the tails. (Leader tape used for the tail of a program is often called *trailer* tape.) Commonly accepted color schemes use white or green to signify the beginning of the program ("heads") and yellow or red to signify the end ("tails"). Obviously, a tape that is would tails-out must be rewound before it can be played back.

DUBBING

Dubbing is the process of making a copy of a recording by playing it back on one machine while recording it on another. Here are some reasons why you'd dub a tape:

- To preserve the original (*master*) copy of any recording. (Always make a copy of any irreplaceable program and store the original in a safe place.)
- To retain an unedited copy of any "raw" recordings for later use.
- To distribute a program to other facilities.
- To enable us to re-process, or "clean up," recordings with audio problems (e.g., equalizing for hum, or evening out erratic levels).
- To provide a full- or half-track open-reel copy of a cassette recording
- To electronically edit.

The term "dubbing" is also used in film sound in two completely different ways:

1. To "dub" can mean to change the language in which the film's dialogue is spoken.
2. To "dub" can refer to the sound mixing process.

ELECTRONIC EDITING

Electronic editing allows us to remove or rearrange portions of a program by *dubbing* only those portions of program material we wish to keep, in the order we wish to keep them. Electronic editing only works with tape machines that make no electronic noise (clicks or pops) on the tape when they start or stop.

Simple electronic editing can be done directly from one tape machine to another. When we want to combine (mix) portions of several recordings (and possible other sound sources) into one "final" recording, we need to use a mixing console.

KEY TERMS TO REMEMBER

china marker (grease pencil)	raw tape
cut-and-splice editing	splice
dubbing	splice editing
electronic editing	splicing block
heads out	splicing tape
leader tape	tails out
master copy	trailer tape

CHAPTER TWENTY–TWO

MIXING

Mixing is combining two or more sound elements so that we hear them simultaneously, and usually at the same time adjusting their relative volumes and processing them as needed. There are several ways to mix sounds together, depending on the effect desired.

METHODS OF MIXING

THE FADE

To *fade* an audio element is to gradually increase or decrease its volume. A *fade-in* is an increase in volume from zero to the level desired; a *fade-out* is the opposite. A *crossfade* is the effect produced by fading out one sound as another is faded in; for a short transition period, both of them are audible.

THE CUT

A *cut* is a sudden transition from one sound element to another; done without fading.

THE BED

A *bed* is an audio element which is heard in the "background" under (behind) another, "foreground" element.

THE COLLAGE

A *collage* is a sound composition of brief consecutive audio elements combined to convey a desired message or image without explanatory narration.

THE MONTAGE

A *montage* is a layering or superimposition of disparate sound elements to convey a single sound image. For example, a montage of a haunted house could mix simultaneously the sounds of wind, thunder, creaking doors, yowling cats, dripping water and screams.

THE BRIDGE

A *bridge* is a sound element used to provide a gradual transition from one program segment to another, often denoting a change in time, space or mood.

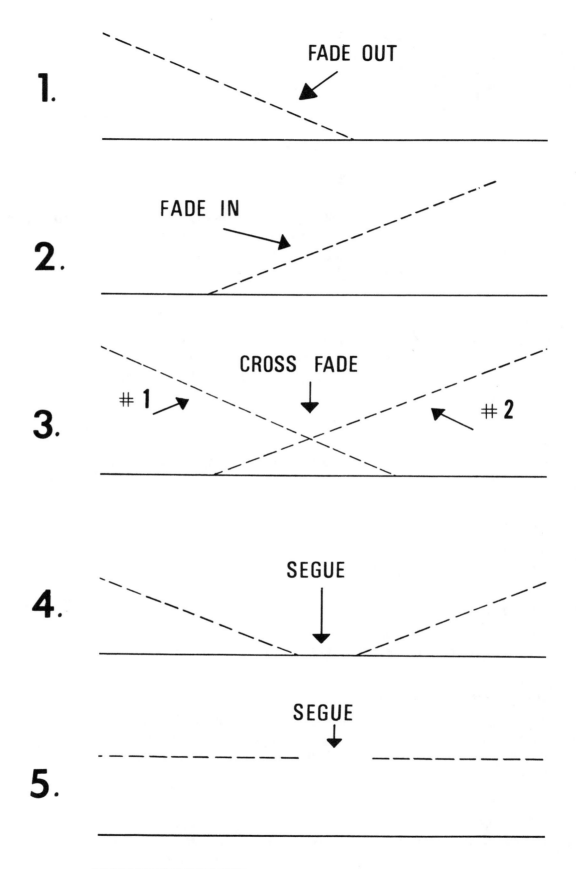

MIXING SOUNDS BY FADING

THE PAN

The *pan* is a stereo effect made by moving a sound to one channel from the other using the pan pot. For example, the sound of a locomotive may be faded up on the left channel, gradually panned to the right channel, and then faded down to create the illusion of a train passing by.

THE SEGUE

Segue (pronounced "seg'-way") is a term borrowed from music to indicate the transition between any two foreground elements or program segments. A segue is made by using a fade, a crossfade or a cut.

Everyone has heard an *echo* at one time or another. Any sound which is reflected, or returned in some other way after a delay, will produce an echo. Using a mixer and three-head tape recorder we can record a sound, "return" it after a short delay, and combine it with our original sound to create an artificial or *tape echo* effect. When we record a sound, it is "placed" on the tape as the tape moves past the recording head. The sound can be reproduced as the tape moves past the playback head a moment later.

In other words, it takes a certain amount of time for the point on the tape at which the sound is recorded to move from the recording head to the playback head. This time lag, or delay, is what we use to produce our tape echo effect. Though all this may sound a bit complex it is quite easy to understand by looking at an illustration of how an echo is produced.

ECHO
(As Done With a Tape Recorder)

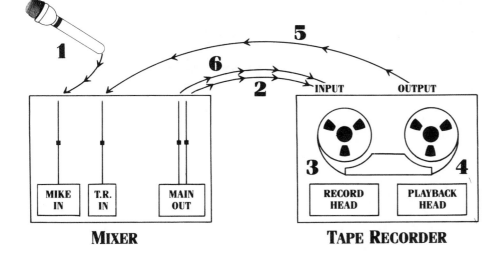

TAPE ECHO

1. With the meter-and-output switch on the tape machine in "PLAYBACK," send a signal to the mixer.
2. This signal is sent to the tape recorder input.
3. This signal is recorded as tape moves past recording head.
4. The signal is reproduced as tape moves past the playback head. (This is where the delay occurs.)
5. The recorded signal is returned to mixer input.
6. This signal gets recorded again a split second later, causing the echo effect.

One way we can vary our echo effect is by increasing or decreasing the delay time. The faster the tape moves between the recording head and the playback head, the shorter our delay time will be. An echo produced with a tape speed of 3¾ ips will have a longer delay than one done at a higher speed.

REVERB

A *reverberation* differs from an echo in two important ways. The delay time of reverberation is much shorter than the delay time of an echo and a reverberation, by definition, is a reflected sound that is repeated more than once (usually hundred or thousands of times in succession so quick that each is not heard separately).

Natural reverberations occur in a *live* acoustic environment, i.e., one that includes highly reflective surfaces. (A *dead* acoustic environment tends to absorb sounds rather than reflect them.) We can roughly approximate a reverberation effect with our tape echo set-up, by using the faster tape speeds. Increasing the volume of the signal returning from the playback head to the mixer will *sustain* our echo effect, causing it to repeat over and over again.

However, this method doesn't provide a totally realistic reverb effect. It can be helpful in creating special effects for conveying certain audio illusions (see "Equalization for Effect"). On the other hand, tape echo/reverb can be easily overused, which can be annoying, so we suggest it be used very sparingly. Refer to Chapter 18 Artificial Reverberation in this book.

KEY TERMS TO REMEMBER

bed	fade-out
bridge	live acoustic environment
collage	montage
crossfade	pan
cut	reverberation
dead acoustic environment	segue
echo	tape echo effect
fade	voice-over
fade-in	

CHAPTER TWENTY-THREE

CONSIDERATIONS IN PROGRAM PRODUCTION

There are two basic kinds of audio production, "real time" and "non-real time." A *non-real-time* mix means bringing together all the sound elements to be used in a program (live voices, records, pre-recorded tapes, etc.) into a studio/control room to mix into a final program. When a mistake is made, the part of the mix containing the mistake can be done over and over again until it's right. The only constraints on the production are the amount of studio time available and the schedules of the people involved.

But in a *real-time* production, there is no opportunity to correct mistakes. The two kinds of real-time productions are: programs broadcast "live" as they happen; and recordings of events (like concerts or panel discussions) which may not be "live" on the air, but nevertheless can't be interrupted for "retakes." Multi-track recording is often used in this last kind of situation because it at least allows for some remixing to happen after the event is over.

Obviously, there is less risk involved in doing non-real-time productions. On the other hand, real-time programs can be much more exciting (when everything goes well!). Our advice is to gain as much experience as possible doing non-real-time productions before attempting the other kind.

REAL-TIME VS. NON-REAL-TIME PRODUCTIONS

TECHNICAL STANDARDS

- *Frequency response*: the reproduction of the high, low and middle frequencies should be consistently accurate.

- *Signal-to-noise*: the level of noise (hiss, buzz, unwanted ambient sound) should be low enough so as not to distract attention from the program.

- *Dynamic range*: the difference in level between the loud and quiet parts of the program should sound as natural as possible.

AESTHETIC CONSIDERATIONS

- How long will the program be? (All introductory remarks, the program itself, and all remarks and credits at the end of the program should be within the time allotted you.)

- What sound elements will the program include? (Music, narration, interviews, actualities, drama, poetry, discussion, ambience, sound effects, etc.)

PRIMARY CONSIDERATIONS IN PROGRAM PRODUCTION

- Will the program be mono or stereo? (Realistic stereo programs can be harder to produce for many reasons, the most salient of which is that the program must sound good in stereo *and* in mono.)
- What will the pace of the program be?
- What "special effects" (reverberation, echo, equalization, panning, montage, collage, etc.) might be useful and where?

DIVISION OF LABOR

In order to produce a complex program, many people will be needed to do the many different kinds of work involved. The three most common jobs are:

- *Producer*: This is the person who is ultimately responsible for making decisions about the nature of the program and whose responsibility it is to bring together and organize all the others working in the project.
- *Technician*: This is a person who operates the equipment involved in making the program.
- *Talent*: This is a traditional radio term for the person who is heard on the air as a part of the program. Actors, musicians, announcer, guests and hosts are all "talent"

Producing audio using the work of several people involves complex ego interactions, is often done under extreme time pressure, and usually requires using facilities which are tightly scheduled. Cooperative productions can be wonderful, but they are best accomplished by a group of people who have already learned to work well together, and have defined their roles and responsibilities.

In many cases, though, a complex production is put together by a group that hasn't had the chance to develop these skills. It is often better to entrust the major decisions and coordination to a single experienced producer than to expend too much energy on cooperative decision-making. Scripts need to be written, talent contacted, recording dates and technical arrangements taken care of, aesthetic decisions made, and publicity arranged and produced.

At any rate, it is sometimes wise to have a program "in the can" (completely finished) before it's even scheduled for broadcast, rather that do a mediocre job (or worse) because of unrealistic time constraints.

PLANNING THE RECORDING SESSION

1. Make sure you have a pretty complete idea of what you want to accomplish in the session *before* you even arrange for the use of the facility (control room or studio). This is because the specific production plans will determine what equipment you'll need.

2. If the session is to consist of mixing more than a few program elements, a *cue sheet* should be prepared which describes the entire mix in detail. This will help any other technicians understand the job more quickly, and will give you as producer a chance to clarify in your own mind any aspects of the mix which haven't yet been well thought out.

3. Show your cue sheet to any technicians who'll be working with you. Ask what they think about the technical feasibility of your ideas. Discuss any

problems (buzz, hiss, distortion, level problems, etc.) that may exist in pre-recorded elements of the production, and how they can be dealt with.

4. Schedule the use of the production facility. Be sure to notify everyone who will need to be there. Make sure that all of the equipment you need will be there at the appointed time.

5. Make sure that any pre-recorded elements are fully prepared *before* the session begins. (In other words, don't begin an hour late because you still have to edit one of the interviews to be used.)

KEY TERMS TO REMEMBER

cue sheet

non-real-time production

producer

real-time production

talent

technician

Basic Production One: "Spots"

One of the most common types of radio production work is the "spot announcement." *Spots* can include: "in-house" regular or special program promos, concert and benefit announcements, special or "novelty" station IDs, program *intros* and *outros*, and public service announcements (PSAs) for outside (non-profit) organizations.

Spots can range from very simple voice-over-music productions to elaborate mini-dramas. They are most often very short (under a minute or so), self-contained pieces, which make them good projects for beginning producers to sharpen their skills. Because they're short and usually designed to be played fairly often, spots are dubbed onto carts at many stations.

Here's an example of a basic, produced PSA (public service announcement) using a musical bed and voice-over.

1. Instrumental music begins at a normal listening level.

2. Music is faded down (but not out) after a few seconds.

3. Voice is brought in with announcement at normal levels, as the music continues "underneath" the announcement as a bed. (The musical bed should be loud enough to be distinctly audible, but soft enough so as not to distract attention from the announcement.)

4. At end of announcement ("voice out"), music fades back up to normal level.

5. After a few seconds, music fades down and out.

It takes some experience to effectively produce even a simple mix like this one. Controlling such factors as the length, speed and depth of fades, the right balance between music and voice levels, and good timing is something best learned by doing it yourself, often.

There are a few tips which can help you produce good spots:

■ It's usually best to use instrumental music for voice-over announcements. Vocal passages tend to compete with the announcement itself for the listener's attention.

■ Music with a wide dynamic range can "disappear" during softer passages when already faded down for a voice-over.

■ Don't let the music play for too long before the voice-over begins. You don't want it to sound as though you are "interrupting" a musical piece in the middle with your announcement.

There are really no hard and fast rules regarding spot production. For instance, sometimes using a well-timed vocal piece with relevant lyrics can add some nice pizazz to the announcement. This sort of production can be much more elaborate, of course, depending on the application. With practice, you can learn how to effectively use different voices, overdubbing more than one piece of music, sound effects, and the like.

KEY TERMS TO REMEMBER

intro   spot
outro

Basic Production Two: Documentaries

One type of program where we can apply all of what we've learned about audio production work is the *documentary*. A documentary uses two or more of the following audio elements in "telling its story:"

- Narration
- Interviews
- Related music
- *Actualities* (sounds related to the subject, recorded "on-the-spot")
- Drama (poetry, skits, readings, etc.)
- Discussion
- Ambience and special effects

THE PRODUCER'S MIX

The key to making a good documentary (as with most types of audio programs) is to avoid doing a "producer's mix." This is a program which is perfectly enjoyable to the producer, who is intensely interested in the subject and has heard all of the elements of the program scores of times, but tends not to be so enjoyable or understandable to listeners hearing the program only once over the air.

Producers may be so involved with the content of the program that they don't realize that:

- Some of the recorded elements are noisy or hard to listen to.
- The subject hasn't been introduced comprehensively for those who are not particularly familiar with it.
- Extraneous information is included.
- The narration contains "uh's" and mispronunciations.
- The elements of the program aren't put together in a logical, easily-understood sequence.
- The program is too long.
- Not enough actualities or music have been used to give the program a varied, attention-getting sound.

- Key points are not repeated or summarized often enough.

- The program is "over-produced" (i.e., too much "related music," too many special effects, too much fast cutting between elements, etc.).

Overproduction tends to sound trite, silly, or unnecessarily slick, and in general trivializes the subject.

STEP-BY-STEP CHRONOLOGY OF A DOCUMENTARY PRODUCTION

What follows is a fairly detailed, step-by-step description of the entire process of producing a taped documentary which contains most of the primary kinds of audio elements and processes. This scenario will give the beginning producer an idea of everything involved in putting together a radio program, besides just the technical end.

PLANNING

First comes the idea. It occurs to me that the subject of surreptitious audio surveillance (bugging) would be interesting, educational, and lend itself well to a radio documentary. Now I must ask myself several questions:

1. Who can work on the project with me, as co-producers or helpers?

2. Has a similar documentary been done before? If so, I should listen to it so that I won't duplicate it and because it will suggest possibilities and problems that may not have occurred to me.

3. What will the focus of the program be? Bugging by government? By private investigators? The equipment used? Legal implications? Political implications? Invasion of privacy? In other words, how will I limit my topic?

4. What is the target audience? Local or national? The general public or a particular segment of it?

5. What are possible sources of information on the subject?

6. How much does the audience already know about the subject?

7. How long should it be?

8. What audio elements can be used to illustrate the subject? Interviews? Music? Actualities? Drama? Narration? Discussion? Special effects?

9. What will be the concerns of my employers (assuming I am not an independent producer)?

10. How long will it take to produce?

11. What will it cost? And who will pay for it?

A friend expresses interest in working as a co-producer. We meet, and come up with these answers to the above questions:

1. The two of us will produce the program.

2. A similar documentary has been produced by the Canadian Broadcasting Corporation. We make arrangements to listen to it.

3. We decide to concentrate on government bugging, and to touch on each of the other related subjects mentioned.

4. The program will be produced primarily for broadcast on the radio station at which we work, but will be adapted for national distribution if it is successful.

5. Our sources of information will be government statistics, magazine articles and books on the topic, and interviews with experts, practitioners and victims.

6. It will be tailored for an audience which knows very little about the subject.

7. We decide that it will take an hour-long program to cover the subject.

8. We intend to use all of the possible audio elements to illustrate the subject.

9. We talk to the program director of the radio station about the project and learn that the station's main concerns are:
   - That there be no libel, obscenity or copyright infringements in the program.
   - That we don't overtax the station's production facilities and tape supplies.
   - That the program be subject to review before it is scheduled to be broadcast.

We estimate it will take about 90 hours of work:
■ Finding and reading informational materials	20 hours
■ Discussion and planning	10 hours
■ Doing outside-of-station recording (actualities)	20 hours
■ Editing	20 hours
■ Studio recording and mixing	20 hours

The work will be spread out over a two-month period. To our amazement, all of the major costs will be covered by the radio station through a programming grant:
■ 15 hours of blank tape, reels, etc.	$200.00
■ Use of station equipment (gauged by cost of renting similar facilities)	2000.00
■ Labor (both yours and station technicians')	2000.00
■ Purchase of materials (magazines, books, etc.)	100.00
■ Phone costs	200.00
■ Non-music talent	400.00
■ Hiring musicians	400.00
■ Travel	200.00

These costs come to a total of $5500.

Since this is a station project, the use of facilities, station labor, station tape and station phones is not a real, added expense (this is called instead an "in-kind" expense). This reduces the "real" cost to an estimated $1100.

After we've discussed all of this, it's time to make specific production plans. I go to the library to find articles and books written on the subject, while my co-producer makes some initial phone calls (to private investigators, police, government agencies, etc.). These calls will help determine who we interview. (We ask each person to suggest other sources of information.)

At our next meeting, we exchange the information garnered from the library and from the phone calls. We decide that three of the people contacted should be interviewed on tape and that both of us will participate in the interviews.

We work out the specific questions we want to ask. We find out when the production room is available. When we make our appointments, we discover that one person can come to the station to be recorded, but that the others will have to be recorded over the phone. We reserve the facilities for the appointed times.

THE INTERVIEW

The first interview will be with the person who is coming to the station. For this interview, we will need three microphones—one for each of the participants. The recording will be mixed in mono, and put on one track of a half-track recorder. During the final mix this track will be mixed to both tracks of the final half-track tape, so that it will be compatible with the stereo elements of the program, which obviously will be on both tracks. You don't record this interview in stereo because you decide that no useful purpose would be served by having the participants on separate channels.

We decide to record on the tape stock for which the station's machines are already biased. We decide not to use noise reduction in the documentary because the dynamic range of the program will not be very great, so tape hiss shouldn't be a problem. (We might have wanted to use a noise reduction device if available, if there were going to be some very quiet passages.) We decide to record the interviews at 15 ips to make editing easier. (The faster the tape moves, the larger the spaces between the words on the tape, so splicing isn't so hard. If our supply of tape were limited we would record at 7½ ips.)

We make and listen to a test recording of the three of us talking, making sure that the mic placement is good, there are no popping "p's," no hum or buzz, the levels are even and as high as possible with no distortion, the signal-to-noise ratio is good, and the frequency response is flat. In other words, the playback signal is nearly identical to the input signal.

We tell the person being interviewed not to worry about making mistakes because they can be easily edited out. (The ideal way to correct oneself when recording on tape, incidentally, is to pause for two or three seconds, and then repeat the sentence in which the mistake was made. This makes things much easier for the tape editor.) When the tape is rolling, the technician points to me and I begin the interview.

The first few minutes are spent making the person being interviewed feel comfortable, since someone who isn't used to microphones may feel a little uncomfortable talking into one. (Of course, in this particular documentary our experts should be quite familiar with them!) During the course of the interview my partner and I must remember not to speak while our interviewee is speaking. It is natural to respond verbally in a conversation even when a verbal response isn't necessary. Our "uh-huh"s and "I see"s will make editing more difficult. We learn to nod our heads creatively.

THE PHONE INTERVIEW

In this set-up, our voices will be picked up by the studio microphones, and sent through the console to the tape recorder and the telephone. We'll be recorded with normal studio quality. But since the other person's voice is coming over a phone line, we may want to improve its quality by running it through an equalizer to boost the bass and treble frequencies.

If there is a bad connection (with a lot of noise or level problems), hang up and try for a better connection. All three signals (voices) will be mixed and sent, mono, to one track of a half-track recorder, just as in the other interview.

EDITING

Now we begin editing. We may want to make copies (dubs) of the interviews and edit the copies, leaving the originals intact. Having several empty reels on hand while editing will allow us to divide the interviews into several parts, each part being stored on its own reel. The most likely basis for organizing the parts is subject matter. For instance, I may put all of the questions and answers on the subject of equipment on one reel, the ones about the history of bugging on another reel, and so on.

The information contained in these interviews may, to a great extent, determine the direction and scope of the program. During this first round of editing, we will also be separating the material which we're likely to use from that which doesn't seem promising. We'll make a *log* of the contents of each reel and keep it in the tape box. These logs will be important in later editing.

ACTUALITIES

Another element we decide to use is a recording of a simulated bugging. My partner asks one of the "experts" to surreptitiously record one of us, later dubbing it to open reel tape, editing and logging it for use as an actuality in the final mix.

DISCUSSION

In our research we find that the station has a recording of a panel discussion that happened at a local university several years ago on the necessity of government wiretapping. Listening to this tape, I find that it contains several heated arguments on the subject that I'd like to use in the program. I make copies of the segments I want to use, edit and log them.

MUSIC

Do I want original music by local people or pre-recorded music? Are copyright arrangements for the music needed if the program is distributed to other stations? Should we use music with relevant lyrics, or no lyrics at all? Should the music be funny, or serious? Whole songs or segments? Used throughout the program, or only at the beginning and end (the intro and outro)?

The music to use in a documentary is music that contributes to the overall thrust of the program. Wisely-used music can add its own editorial comment, but poor use of music can spoil the desired impact of a program.

In this case, we decide to use part of a song called "Big Brother's Watching" from a record by a popular group, at the beginning and end of the program, and some instrumental music by a local group for segues within the program.

The piece on the album is dubbed to tape during the final mix, but arrangements have to be made to record the original instrumental music in the studio.

We decide to record the music in stereo. There will be a snare drum, an acoustic guitar and a bass fiddle. We want the guitar to be louder on one track (the right), the bass to be louder on the other (the left), and the drum to be of equal volume on both tracks (which will make it sound in the "center" when reproduced in stereo). One cardioid mic is used to "close mic" each instrument, which will allow you to pick up as much of the direct, "pure" sound of the instruments, and as little of the "room sound," as possible.

NARRATION

At this point, we must decide on the final "lay-out" of the program, and write the narration (*continuity*). As the nature of the sound elements we have will determine the content of the narration, so will the form of the narration determine how we arrange the sound elements. After the narration is written, it is recorded. It's usually much easier to work with taped narration in the final mix than with live narration.

THE CUE SHEET

Now that all of the elements of the program are on tape, a schematic diagram (cue sheet) of the entire production is necessary to organize the mix of the elements *before* we go into the studio. Invariably, a few changes will be made in the control room, but it's not a good idea to go in without a plan unless there is no deadline to meet and frustration is a good time.

There are lots of ways to make a cue sheet, but one of the easiest to understand and read is a graphic representation of the mix, with each element represented by a different color or symbol (dots, dashes, etc.). In this way, the levels can be displayed and special effects penciled in next to the elements on which they are to be used *and* for the exact duration of time they are to be used.

The segments you see in the illustration represent about five minutes of two hypothetical mixes. Once all of the elements are assembled and cued, one might reasonably expect to spend thirty minutes to an hour on the mixing of just these two segments!

THE FINAL MIX

Your job in the final mixing session is to combine all of the sound elements according to the plan outlined in your cue sheet.

The segues can be accomplished either by splicing or electronic editing. Since some of the elements in the program are stereo, however, the mono elements will have to be dubbed onto both tracks of the final tape. Be sure to listen to the final mix once in mono to catch any phase cancellation problems that may occur. You should also listen once to your final mix on a small, low-fi speaker, which is how many listeners will hear the program. Audio segments which work well when listened to in high fidelity can become lost when heard on a home table radio or car radio.

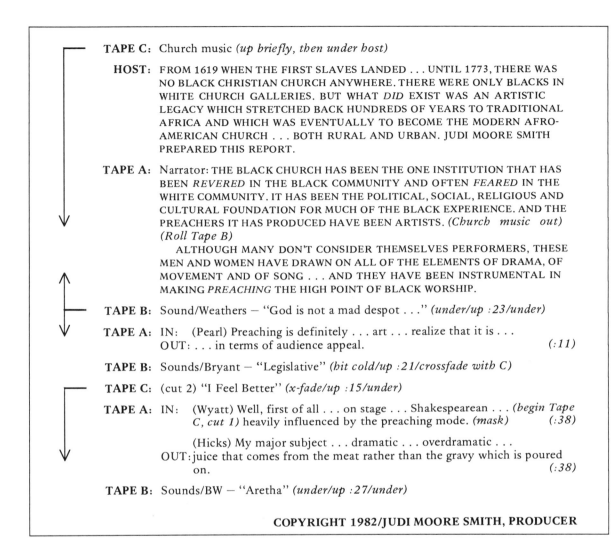

TAPE C: Church music (*up briefly, then under host*)

HOST: FROM 1619 WHEN THE FIRST SLAVES LANDED . . . UNTIL 1773, THERE WAS NO BLACK CHRISTIAN CHURCH ANYWHERE. THERE WERE ONLY BLACKS IN WHITE CHURCH GALLERIES. BUT WHAT *DID* EXIST WAS AN ARTISTIC LEGACY WHICH STRETCHED BACK HUNDREDS OF YEARS TO TRADITIONAL AFRICA AND WHICH WAS EVENTUALLY TO BECOME THE MODERN AFRO-AMERICAN CHURCH . . . BOTH RURAL AND URBAN. JUDI MOORE SMITH PREPARED THIS REPORT.

TAPE A: Narrator: THE BLACK CHURCH HAS BEEN THE ONE INSTITUTION THAT HAS BEEN *REVERED* IN THE BLACK COMMUNITY AND OFTEN *FEARED* IN THE WHITE COMMUNITY. IT HAS BEEN THE POLITICAL, SOCIAL, RELIGIOUS AND CULTURAL FOUNDATION FOR MUCH OF THE BLACK EXPERIENCE. AND THE PREACHERS IT HAS PRODUCED HAVE BEEN ARTISTS. (*Church music out*) (*Roll Tape B*)
ALTHOUGH MANY DON'T CONSIDER THEMSELVES PERFORMERS, THESE MEN AND WOMEN HAVE DRAWN ON ALL OF THE ELEMENTS OF DRAMA, OF MOVEMENT AND OF SONG . . . AND THEY HAVE BEEN INSTRUMENTAL IN MAKING *PREACHING* THE HIGH POINT OF BLACK WORSHIP.

TAPE B: Sound/Weathers — "God is not a mad despot . . ." (*under/up :23/under*)

TAPE A: IN: (Pearl) Preaching is definitely . . . art . . . realize that it is . . .
OUT: . . . in terms of audience appeal. (*:11*)

TAPE B: Sounds/Bryant — "Legislative" (*hit cold/up :21/crossfade with C*)

TAPE C: (cut 2) "I Feel Better" (*x-fade/up :15/under*)

TAPE A: IN: (Wyatt) Well, first of all . . . on stage . . . Shakespearean . . . (*begin Tape C, cut 1*) heavily influenced by the preaching mode. (*mask*) (*:38*)

(Hicks) My major subject . . . dramatic . . . overdramatic . . .
OUT: juice that comes from the meat rather than the gravy which is poured on. (*:38*)

TAPE B: Sounds/BW — "Aretha" (*under/up :27/under*)

COPYRIGHT 1982/JUDI MOORE SMITH, PRODUCER

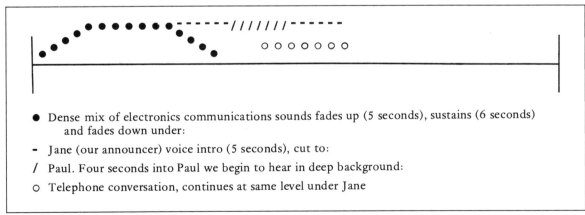

- Dense mix of electronics communications sounds fades up (5 seconds), sustains (6 seconds) and fades down under:
- Jane (our announcer) voice intro (5 seconds), cut to:
/ Paul. Four seconds into Paul we begin to hear in deep background:
o Telephone conversation, continues at same level under Jane

TWO SAMPLE CUE SHEETS

There is no established convention for formatting a cue sheet. Some producers use primarily narrative means to script out their production; some diagram it graphically. Most producers have developed their own styles that combine elements of narrative and diagram.

Above are two sample cue sheets. The first is excerpted from a piece by Judi Moore Smith on Black preaching, and the second diagrams a breif segment of our program on wiretapping.

When the program is finished, label both the reels and the boxes containing it. Information on the labels should include: program title; length (time); speed; whether it is wound to the beginning or end of the program ("heads" or "tails"); mono or stereo; track configuration; whether it is part of an integral program contained on more than one reel (e.g., "reel 1 of 3"); the name of the producer; and the date produced.

KEY TERMS TO REMEMBER

actualities
continuity
documentary
features

in-kind expense
log
room tone

BASIC PRODUCTION THREE: REMOTES

Remote refers to some type of production which occurs outside of the station's own facilities. Remotes can be broadcast live, or they can be recorded (and edited) for later use, or both. Broadcast remotes are more complex, as they necessitate the use of some kind of equipment to get the signal from the remote site to the station.

In this chapter, we'll be discussing live remotes for broadcast, though the actual mixing and recording of an event is much the same regardless of whether it's broadcast live or not. There are two ways to send a signal from a remote location back to the station. One uses telephone lines, and the other uses a portable radio transmitter (*Remote Pickup Unit*) at the site of the event, which sends a signal to a special receiver at the station.

TELEPHONE TRANSMISSION

A signal can be sent by phone lines from a remote site back to the station using either a *dial-up line* or a *dedicated line*. These lines can be either *equalized* or *unequalized*.

"DIAL-UP" LINES

This method is the cheapest, and may be completely adequate for some applications (e.g., short news feeds), but it provides the poorest quality signal. Use a standard telephone to call from the remote site, and send the signal into the phone line, bypassing the telephone's low-quality microphone.

The signal can come from the output of a tape recorder, a mixing console, or a microphone, but the method of connecting the output to the telephone is basically the same. The only special connector needed for this type of transmission can be made for a few dollars. At one end of a cable are attached two *alligator clips*, and at the other whatever plug is needed to mate with the output of the signal source. A normal portable cassette recorder is often used as a signal for this kind of remote. Here is a step-by-step guide:

1. Unscrew the mouthpiece from the phone and pull out the disc-shaped microphone.

2. Attach one of the alligator clips to each of the two metal contacts which lie under the mic. It doesn't matter which clip is on which contact, as long as they don't touch.

3. Connect the plug at the other end of the cable to the "monitor" jack of the cassette machine. (This will usually be a "mini" connector.)

4. Plug a mic into the mic jack of the recorder.

5. Put a cassette tape into the recorder and put the machine into recording mode.

6. Dial the radio station.

7. Now speak into the mic instead of the telephone's mouthpiece, while listening through the telephone's earpiece as usual.

All you're doing here is avoiding the telephone's very poor mic. The cassette machine is acting as a pre-amplifier for your microphone.

With this same set-up, pre-recorded actualities (interviews, related sound, etc.) can also be sent to the station, by simply depressing the recorder's "PLAY" button instead of "RECORD." Many cassette recorders are built so that you can put the machine in the "recording" mode *without* engaging the transport and actually recording on the tape. In this case, you can alternate between a "live mic" feed and pre-taped feeds very quickly with just a little practice. Be careful to disengage the recording mode before putting the machine in "PLAY," so as not to erase your pre-recorded tape.

Send a sample of program material "down the line" to the station so the technician there can check the quality and adjust the recording levels. We can further improve the quality of a signal sent over a "dial-up" line by equalizing it at the station. (Dial-up lines tend to be noisy, with lots of hum and buzz.)

Connecting a dial-up line to audio equipment at the station requires the use of a *phone coupling device*. Don't connect the phone directly to equipment in the station without the help of an engineer. There are high levels of *direct current (DC)* electricity in dial-up phone lines that can damage the inputs of tape recorders and other equipment.

"DEDICATED" PHONE LINES

A "dedicated" phone line (also called a *broadcast loop* or *cable pair*) uses only the telephone company's wires, while you supply the equipment at both ends of the line (at the remote site and at the station), bypassing the use of any telephones at all. A dedicated line is a higher-quality circuit, and much quieter than a normal dial-up line.

You can order a dedicated phone line installation for just about anywhere in your local phone company's service area, but the cost will vary with the distance between the remote site and the station. You should order the line at least two weeks in advance of the scheduled remote broadcast. If possible, be sure to test the line one "working" day before the broadcast, so the phone company can be notified in case there are any problems with the line.

INTERFACING WITH THE PHONE COMPANY EQUIPMENT

Most of our studio equipment operates with an output impedance of 600 Ω (ohms). Unfortunately, most telephone lines operate at a different (usually lower) impedance. For this reason, we'll need to use an *impedance matching transformer* at each end of the dedicated line, which will also serve to match the levels between your audio equipment and the phone company equipment. One transformer is connected between our audio equipment and the phone line at the remote site, and the other between the phone line and the audio equipment at the station.

Once the phone line is installed, you'll want to check it out before the scheduled broadcast date, so you can notify the phone company if there are any problems. There are almost always problems, and they can be put in three categories:

■ A good signal isn't getting to the phone company's transformer at the remote site. This is a job for the remote crew.

■ A good signal *is* getting to that transformer but *not* to the transformer at the station.

■ A good signal is getting to the station transformer but not to the on-air board. This is a job for the station crew.

If the station isn't receiving a high-quality signal, the problem lies in one *or more* of these three areas. The first line of action is for the remote and station crews to check all of their connections and patches. If everything seems okay, then it's time to call the phone company.

DEALING WITH THE PHONE COMPANY

The most important thing to remember when dealing with the phone company is that very few people there will have had much experience with providing broadcast phone line service. When you order a dedicated line, make sure the ordering department knows *exactly* what you're talking about. Most phone companies have a specialized department (usually called something like "program services") for providing out-of-the-ordinary services like broadcast lines. Once you've developed a contact with a competent person in this department, always try to order phone lines through that person.

Likewise, you should develop a working relationship with the phone company technicians who know how to install and maintain broadcast phone lines. In many cities, you can request that the phone company send a particular technician (who has worked with your station before) to install your lines. A sympathetic and knowledgeable person working with you on a regular basis is a very valuable resource, helping you to cut through the labyrinthine bureaucracy of the phone company.

Quite often, this technician will be willing to offer you personal advice and assistance with your broadcast line—something you could never get by calling up "customer assistance." (Imagine trying to find out what they feed the guard dogs at the local Air Force base by calling the general information number at the Pentagon.)

Phone company problems always seem to happen during a live event, at night, or on a weekend when all your carefully-cultivated personal contacts are not available to help you. In this emergency situation, you are forced to deal with the "repair service" department. here are some tips which can help you make the best of this undesirable situation:

■ Every broadcast dedicated line ("cable pair") will be assigned its own special ID number by the phone company. MAKE SURE YOU KNOW WHAT THESE NUMBERS ARE! The technician who installs the line can give them to you.

■ When you call the service number, inform the operator immediately that you need help with a *broadcast* line. Ask for "program services" (or whatever that department is called in your town).

■ If you can't get through to program services, ask to be connected to the "test board." Most phone companies have a qualified technician on duty there 24 hours a day.

■ Give the test board technician your broadcast line ID numbers, then explain exactly what problems you are having.

■ Make sure the test board person has a number where you can be reached.

■ Give the test board technician the name of the technician who installed your line. (He or she may be able to be contacted and suggest where to track down the problem.

■ If the worst happens, and you are unable to salvage the broadcast, you will at least not have to pay for the dedicated line. Make sure a report is filled out by the phone company technicians, and contact the billing office on the next business day to make sure you're not charged. Even if you go ahead with the broadcast despite noise problems or intermittent connections, you can still demand that you not be charged. Make sure you notify the phone company when the problem occurs, so they can verify it for themselves.

EQUALIZATION

A dedicated line, though quieter than a dial-up line, will not always have significantly better frequency response. Equalizing the line at the station can improve the sound quality tremendously and, in many cases, provide a truly high fidelity transmission. A typical unequalized phone line only passes the midrange frequencies —from 400 to 3,500 Hz. We improve the fidelity by boosting the lows and highs, and attenuating the midrange.

"Seat of the pants" equalization is often sufficient for voice-quality broadcasts. Have someone speak (or send program material) through the equipment at the remote site. Send this signal through your equalizer at the station, and adjust the EQ controls until the audio sounds right.

If you need high fidelity (flat response), though, you'll need to have someone send tones down the line from the remote site with an audio tone generator. Send one tone at a time, starting with a low frequency, say 50 Hz. Each succeeding tone should be twice the frequency of the previous tone: thus, in this example, 50 Hz, 100 Hz, 200, 400, 800 1.6 kHz, 3.2 kHz, and so on up to 15 kHz. Each tone must be sent *at the same level*—for example zero VU— as all the others.

At the station, route this signal through your equalizer to some device with a good VU meter. Adjust the equalizer until each tone registers at the same level on the meter as the other tones, i.e., until the frequency response is flat across the entire audio spectrum. In other words, if the 200 Hz tone reads zero VU on your meter, the other frequency tones should also read zero VU.

Send this tone sequence down the line several times, until the frequency response is as flat as possible.

This is also a good time to send a signal down the line from the remote board to the station to match your levels—you want a zero VU level on the remote mixing board to give a corresponding zero VU level on the station broadcast board. Rerun these tests and double check these settings shortly before the broadcast begins.

If it isn't possible to provide your own equalization, you can order a broadcast-quality equalized line from the phone company. These are significantly more expensive, however, as the phone company will be providing their EQ equipment and setting it up for you.

In short, the higher the quality of the line, the more it will cost. Most phone companies offer two steps in quality of equalized lines: *5 kHz lines* and *15 kHz lines*. (These refer to the upper limit of frequencies which can be transmitted through the lines.)

A 5 kHz line is sufficient for most "voice-quality" remotes (panel discussions, sporting events, etc.). The audio for many network radio broadcasts is sent over the equivalent of a 5 kHz line. But high quality remote broadcasts of music events necessitate the use of the costlier 15 kHz line.

So far, we've been talking about using only one telephone line at a time. Stereo broadcasts will, of course, require using two separate lines, one for each channel.

If you are doing a stereo remote, check the phase relationship between the two phone lines. An easy way to do this is by summing the output of the two phone lines, running the same level signal through both of them, and listening to them in mono at the station. If the level drops noticeably when you switch your monitor to mono, reverse the two wires on *one* of the phone lines to correct the phase problem.

REMOTE PICKUP UNITS (RPUs)

Remote pickup units are portable radio transmitters which are used most often to send live events from remote locations (concert halls, public meeting places, demonstrations, etc.) back to the radio station. An RPU transmitter has a line level audio input, into which the output of a portable board or tape recorder can be plugged. The transmitter sends the audio signal to a special receiver at the station, by means of an antenna pointed in the direction of the station's special receiving antenna.

Some RPUs are equipped with a built-in mixer, into which mics can be directly plugged. High-quality RPUs can cost several thousand dollars, have excellent frequency response, and offer very high fidelity.

Your station has to get a special license from the FCC to operate an RPU. They operate on one of two radio bands: 150-160 *megaHertz* (million Hertz), and 450-455 mHz. Since both of these bands are used for other kinds of communications (two-way business paging, for example), there is a chance, mainly in large cities, of interference by other transmissions on the same frequencies.

Another possible drawback to the use of RPUs is if large buildings or hills are present between the RPU and the receiving antenna at the station. Such obstructions can cause noisy transmission, or prevent it entirely.

Advantages of RPUs over phone line transmission include:

- They can be used *anywhere* there is a power source (and some can even be battery-operated), giving you much greater mobility.
- You don't have to deal with the phone company.
- They can be used on the spur of the moment.

When using an RPU, send a signal with it from your proposed remote site to the station well in advance of the event, to make sure you can get a good signal. This is called an *RF (radio frequency) shot*. The signal from a high-quality RPU should not need to be equalized.

DOING A LIVE REMOTE MUSIC BROADCAST

Most music remotes are big jobs. Some preliminary considerations:

- Are there enough people to help carry and watch equipment? Will the station be able to continue important production work lacking the equipment you are taking to the remote site? Can at least one highly experienced technician be present at both the remote and station ends? The answer to *all* of these questions must be "Yes" before you continue planning for a remote.
- Is there enough lead time to make all the necessary arrangements? Have the phone lines been ordered, or the remote transmitter tested at the proposed site? Has there been a conference between the technicians (lighting, sound and stage manager) at the facility to be used, and the head technician and producer for the remote?

THE JOBS THAT HAVE TO BE DONE

Producer: The person who is ultimately in charge of the remote. The producer should be at the remote site.

Remote Technician: The person who makes sure all of the equipment gets to the remote site, is set up, works properly, and is operated correctly.

Station Technician: The person who makes sure the signal is being processed correctly at the station end—both the broadcast and any recording which is to take place there. It is essential that someone be at the station who can recognize and fix technical problems that may occur, especially during the pre-event testing.

Announcer(s): At least one person who can speak on the air should be present at the remote site for a live broadcast.

Helpers: People who carry equipment, carry messages, and gopher this or that. Often they are apprentice technicians.

Logger: The person who takes care of the tapes as they are recorded and logs each of the songs played, musicians, times, etc. The log makes processing the tapes much easier later on.

Usually there will not be a different person doing each of these jobs. The producer may announce. The remote technician may do the logging. In fact, for small remotes only two people may be involved, one at the site and one at the station.

THE PA AND YOUR REMOTE

Most music events these days are sent through a public address (*sound reinforcement*) system. One of the biggest problems in doing remote recording or broadcasts is coordinating the PA equipment and the radio station equipment. There are three basic ways this can be done.

Double Miking: Two microphones are pointed at each sound source. One mic from each sound source is plugged into the PA mixer, and the other is plugged into the recording/broadcast mixer.

Advantages:

■ Each set of technicians can do their own mix, with the mics of their choice.

■ The two systems are not connected, and therefore are less likely to cause electrical problems.

Disadvantages:

■ There will be twice as much clutter on stage.

■ Performers may find dealing with two mics confusing or irritating.

■ It is sometimes difficult to effectively mic a sound source (for example, a voice) with two separate mics.

The Feed Technique: Sometimes the radio station technicians will find themselves in a "one-down" relationship with the PA people. This is because the PA people are being paid to make sure that the event sounds good to the live audience who came to hear it. Your equipment (or even your very presence) may seem to them an added complication with which they would rather not deal.

When your station becomes involved in doing a live remote, you should consult with the people running the PA, well in advance of the event. Cooperation will make everybody happier, and the event should run much more smoothly.

Because the PA people want the least amount of hassle with your equipment, they will often suggest that the radio station be "fed" the PA mix through a spare output of the PA board (the "feed" technique).

Advantages:

■ This is often the simplest and quickest method, both in terms of the amount of equipment needed and of the complexity of interconnecting the systems.

Disadvantages:

■ The best PA mix will usually not be the best recording/broadcast mix.

- The person doing the PA mix may be a poor mixer.
- The PA mix will almost always be mono.
- The PA output may not be well-matched, impedance- or level-wise, to the station input. (This, however, can be checked in advance of the event, and any special cables, impedance-matching or level-matching devices that will be needed secured at that time.)

Mic Splitting: In this procedure only one set of mics is used, but they are plugged into a device (a *splitter* box) which "splits" them into two separate sets of outputs going to two separate mixers (PA and recording/broadcast). Sometimes mics can be "split" at the board, since some mixing consoles have a separate mic level output for each mic input. These outputs can be fed via a *squid* or *snake* (one extra-large cable containing many smaller, regular cables) to another board's inputs. This system thus allows two distinct mixes to be made, one for recording/broadcast, and one for PA.

Splitting mics is the way most professional jobs are done, but in order to have time to work out possible electrical problems it is absolutely necessary that there be a test made *at least* three hours before the event is to begin. Anything else is asking for trouble.

Advantages

- Separate PA and recording/broadcast mixes can be done.
- There is less clutter of mics and cables than in double miking.

Disadvantages

- In many cases, connecting two electrical systems in this way will cause what is called a *ground loop*. The result is a buzz in either the PA system, the station system, or both. The two most common ways of attempting to get rid of the buzz are: reversing the power-cord plug at the AC socket; and connecting the *chassis* frames) of various pieces of equipment by means of *clip-wires* to something that actually goes into the ground (a cold water pipe, for instance).
- You may need a "splitter box."

AUDIENCE MICS

Using specially-placed mics to pick up the audience reaction can be effective, but is by no means necessary since the performers' mics often pick up the audience as well as needed. Until you have a lot of experience doing remotes, the time you spend dealing with audience mics would be better spent in making sure the performers' mics are under control.

For audience miking, use one omnidirectional mic if your recording is mono, hung as high as possible over the heads of the audience. In stereo recording, hang two omni mics, one on the left and one on the right of the stage. The audience mics should be *at least* ten times as far away from the performers' mics as those mics are from the performers. Be sure you don't mix the audience mics too high in relation to the performers' mics.

MIC IDENTIFICATION

It is vital to be able to tell which mic on the stage is plugged into which of your board inputs. Simply labeling the pots on the board as "guitar," "piano," "vocal," etc., should certainly be done, but it may not be enough because mics or stands may be moved during the performance.

There are several other ways to more clearly identify the mics or stands themselves. The best and easiest involves wrapping colored tape around the mics, stands or cables, with the number of rings indicating the number of the associated pot.

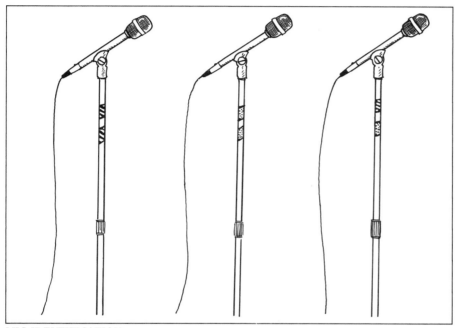

MIC IDENTIFICATION

In this method of identifying which mic is plugged into which volume control on the board, pieces of tape are wrapped around the mic stand. Striped tape stands for "fives" and dotted tape for "ones." Dots and stripes are used here because we don't have color but, in practice, yellow and white adhesive tape would be good choices. They are easy to see and tell apart even in relative darkness and from a distance. The mic identified as "Number Two" is plugged into the second volume control on the board.

Remember that often you will be some distance from the stage and the lights may be dim, so use bright colors and wide rings of tape. All these methods begin to lose their effectiveness as the number of mics becomes larger than eight or ten.

CLOSE MONITORING ON REMOTES

One of the biggest problems in doing remote recordings or broadcasts is that it is often hard to monitor the signal being picked up by the microphones. Many headphones don't reproduce bass frequencies very well, so there may be a hum problem which isn't noticed until you get back to the station and listen through better equipment in a quieter environment. Likewise, headphones may not give an accurate indication of how well the bass frequencies in the *signal* are being picked up.

Still another possible problem with headphones is that when the technician is in the same room as the event being recorded, some of the sound in the room will inevitably leak through the headphones. Since the "room sound" will be different from the sound picked up by the mics, the headphone leakage may make it very hard to determine exactly what the mics are or are not picking up. Some headphones provide much better isolation than others; use those.

Another solution for many of these kinds of problems is for the recording technician, board and tape machine to be in a different room than the event. This makes it possible to use loudspeakers to monitor the signal as it is recorded. But the problem with this is that the recordist (in another room) can't see what is happening on stage.

If you have lots of money, this problem can be overcome by the use of a headset communication device between someone who is in the room with the event, and the recordist. These systems can be bought for several hundred dollars.

But for most of us, headphones have to be used, so they should be loud enough to overcome the leakage problem as much as possible. Many tape recorder and mixer headphone outputs don't supply a sufficiently loud signal to do this; separate headphone amplifiers can be bought in these cases for this purpose.

SOUND CHECKS

A *sound check* or "dress rehearsal" should happen at least a couple of hours before the event. This consists of the musicians playing while the PA and radio people check their mixes. Some things to consider in a sound check are:

- Will the loudest portions of the music overload any of the mic pre-amps?

- What is the order of the pieces to be played, and are there any mic or mixing changes required for them?

- Are there likely to be feedback problems? (This is usually the responsibility of the PA people.)

- Should all of the mics on stage be left "open" (turned up) on the board during the performance? (Usually it is best to leave "on" only those mics which you are sure will be used in a given piece, but if the performers move around a lot or frequently improvise, it may be best to leave all the mics "up" so that nothing is missed.)

- If you are recording the event, which of the instruments should be assigned to which tracks on the tape? (In doing a stereo mix, it is assumed that some of the instruments will be primarily in one channel, some will be primarily in the other, and that some will be at the same level in both channels.)

OTHER HINTS FOR REMOTES

Boom stands are much more versatile than either table or boomless floor stands, and less noisy than *gooseneck* stands.

Avoid using microphones with on-off switches. There is *nothing* you can do at the board if a microphone on stage is switched off during a performance. If you must use a mic with a switch, tape the switch into the "ON" position with some *duct tape* before the event begins.

Always bring lots of duct tape with you on remotes!

Never run mic cables parallel to AC power cords, as this will greatly increase the chance of hum and buzz entering the audio circuits. If any of your cables must cross a power cord, see that it is at a 90 degree angle.

It is always a good idea to secure your cables, once they have been positioned, with duct tape to avoid their being tripped over or accidentally disconnected during a performance. (Remember that they should be placed where there is the least chance of their being stepped on in the first place.) Secure your AC power cord to the socket with duct tape for the same reasons.

Remember that all volume controls should be turned all the way down before turning a power amp on or off.

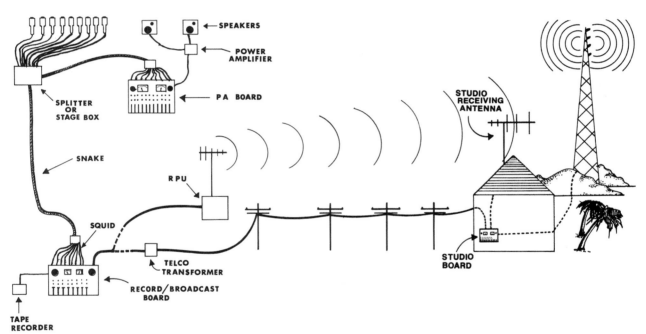

A LIVE REMOTE BROADCAST

This drawing illustrates the main signal paths involved in a live remote broadcast. Two major variables are: 1) the signal may be transmitted from the remote location back to the station either by telephone lines or by a portable radio transmitter (RPU); and 2) the method of mixing to obtain mixes for both the PA system and the radio broadcast depends on the equipment that is available.

STEP-BY-STEP CHRONOLOGY OF A MUSIC REMOTE

AT LEAST TWO WEEKS BEFORE THE EVENT:

■ An estimate of the cost and technical feasibility is made, and a meeting of appropriate station personnel is held to decide whether to do it.

■ Permission of the performers and promoters is obtained.

■ Arrangements are made to rent phone lines, or an "RF shot" is tried from the remote location.

- All of the details for the remote are discussed at a meeting that includes the stage manager of the event, the person(s) who will be doing the PA, the station producer and your remote technicians.
- A station crew is chosen, and meets to discuss details.
- Publicity for the broadcast is arranged.

SEVERAL DAYS BEFORE THE EVENT:

- Checklist is made of all the equipment needed for the remote.
- All equipment to be used is tested, and cables checked for phase problems or intermittent connections.

THE DAY OF THE EVENT:

- Station crew arrives at location at least five hours before a major event (or two hours before a smaller, simple event).
- Phone lines or RPU are given final test, and settings adjusted.
- Mics are set up and cables are run to the board.
- Each mic is tested with its cable, and any problems isolated and solved.
- Tape machines are checked to see if they are recording properly.
- When you finish your set-up, someone should stay with the equipment until the performance for security reasons.
- Taped interviews with the musicians might be done at this point.
- Send someone out for food. After eating, wash your hands!
- At least thirty minutes before the event, all the mics should be in place and all equipment should be checked once more. Make sure the signal from all the mics is reaching the board, and that there are no noise problems.
- Start sending your feed to the station thirty minutes before the show begins so that any changes in the schedule, or equipment adjustments, can be communicated.
- In most cases, the remote announcer goes on the air a few minutes before the scheduled beginning of the event. The announcer can use this time to give the location and details of the event, describe the scene, indicate who will be playing what, ask for subscriptions, do a station ID and so forth.
- While this is happening, all mics except the announcer's should be off or faded down substantially. The board operator should be ready to fade up both the musicians' and audience mics on a second's notice.
- During the sound check, the board operator should have gotten a good idea of where the board pots should be set for the first piece. Without a sound check, don't be surprised if it takes a while to get a good mix, especially when there are more than five or six mics involved.
- After the concert, carefully and quickly pack up your gear. Be sure your equipment doesn't get mixed up with the PA or band equipment. This is also a prime time for theft, so watch your equipment like a hawk.

- Inventory all of your equipment and inspect it for damage once you are back at the station.
- If you've used a phone line, call the phone company and tell them you are done with the line. This is called "goodnighting the line."

KEY TERMS TO REMEMBER

alligator clip	goodnighting the line
boom stand	gooseneck stand
broadcast loop	megaHertz (mHz)
cable pair	phone coupling device
chassis	remote
clip-wire	Remote Pick-up Unit (RPU)
dedicated line	RF (radio frequency) shot
dial-up line	snake
direct current (DC) electricity	sound check
double miking	sound reinforcement system
duct tape	split miking
equalized line	splitter box
feed technique	squid
5 kHz line	unequalized line
15 kHz line	

SOME FINAL WORDS

This manual, like any other, is only a starting point. Experimenting and making plenty of mistakes in the process has always been the least dispensable part of education.

But before you can make mistakes you have to find a place, a working environment in which to make them, a job. The best advice is to look hard for someone to whom you can apprentice. For most of us who would like to work in the media arts there is no "front door," behind which sits the angel to whom we hand our diploma, and who in turn gives us a job. Those who make it inside seem always to have sneaked in through the side or back somehow, and it's as often the blind courage to ask, or a certain look in the eye, or dumb luck that gets that first all-important foot in the door as it is the proper "credentials."

Before you go looking for a mentor, though, think long and hard about exactly what you want to do. You may have this person's ear only once. The two most important qualifications for nearly any job on earth are:

■ enthusiasm about the work

■ tact

If your potential employer has any brains, he or she doesn't care nearly as much about your "credentials" as about what kind of person you are. They will be working and joking and negotiating with you, not your diploma.

Having said all that, it is important to remember that it's foolish not to have as strong a theoretical foundation as possible in your field of interest. Working with different types of equipment, and with different people, is important. The same functions frequently have different names on different brands of equipment, and the same processes are called by different names or done in different ways by different technicians. Learning the "jargon" makes it easier to use equipment and to communicate with others of your (our) ilk.

Don't be afraid of the machines—they're under your control!

GLOSSARY

AC   In electricity, alternating current.

ACETATE   A type of plastic film used as a backing for audio tape, not often used in professional applications because it breaks easily. (Polyester tape or mylar backing tends to stretch rather than break, and is used more often. Acetate is preferable in one way, because a broken piece can usually be spliced back together, whereas the signal on a stretched piece of tape is lost forever.

ACOUSTIC   1. Pertaining to hearing, or to the science of sounds. 2. (In reference to musical performance) A musician or group of musicians playing instruments which are not electrically amplified.

ACOUSTICS   1. The science of sound. 2. The qualities or characteristics of an environment that determine how sounds within it are heard.

ACTUALITY   An "on-the-spot" recording of sound material, usually used with reference to a part of a news or documentary program.

AGC   Automatic Gain Control.

ALC   Automatic Gain Control.

ALKALINE   A type of battery with a longer lifespan than ordinary batteries.

ALLIGATOR CLIP   A connector consisting of a spring clip with serrated teeth (reminiscent of an alligator's jaws), used in making grounding or other temporary connections.

ALTERNATING CURRENT   The type of electrical current which continuously and regularly alternates its direction of flow.

AMBIENCE   All of the "natural sounds" of any environment. The ambience of a tavern, for example, might consist of conversation, laughter, clinking of glasses, music, the hum of the coolers, etc.

AMP   1. See "amplifier." 2. See "ampere."

AMPERE   A unit of electrical current, named after the French physicist, Andre Marie Ampere, Commonly called "amp."

AMPLIFIER   A device which boosts the amplitude of electrical signals; also called "amp."

AMPLIFY   To increase in volume or amplitude; the opposite of "attenuate."

AMPLITUDE   The intensity of a sound wave or electrical current.

ANALOG   A similarity in pattern between one kind of signal and another. For instance, a microphone creates an electrical analog of a sound, and a tape recorder creates a magnetic analog of an electrical signal.

ANTENNA   A metallic structure designed to radiate the radio waves coming from a radio transmitter, or to receive such waves, at a specific frequency or band of frequencies.

ARL   See "automatic gain control."

ATTACK TIME   1. The beginning of any sound, i.e., the length of time necessary for the perception of that sound. Some sounds have a fast attack time (the sound of the spoken letter "t," or most percussion instruments); some have a slower attack time (the sound of the spoken letter "a," or most bowed string instruments. In tape editing, sounds with fast attack times are easier to space closely. 2. In a compressor/limiter, the length of time required for the device to react to a signal which has exceeded the threshold of compression.

ATTENUATE   To reduce in volume or amplitude; the opposite of "amplify."

AUDIO   Pertaining to signals in the audio range.

AUDIO CONSOLE   See "board."

AUDIO OSCILLATOR   See "oscillator."

AUDIO RANGE   The band of frequencies potentially audible to the human ear, usually assumed to be 16 Hz to 20 kHz; also called "audio band" or "audio spectrum."

AUDITION   1. (*verb*) To review some piece of program material before broadcast; to cue. 2. (*noun*) One of the two primary output buses of a broadcast mixing console.

AUTOMATED CONSOLE   A mixing board in which the settings of the principal faders, and sometimes other controls, can be memorized by a computer, and reset to the appropriate positions at any time. For example, if a change needed to be done to a mix which had been completed the previous day, the computer would "remember" the settings of the principal controls at the point of the change, making the fix much easier than it would be without automation. Automation can also be useful in doing complex, multiple fader moves. Instead of trying to move all the faders at once, with automation the moves can be done one fader at a time.

AUTOMATIC GAIN CONTROL   A type of compressor which automatically adjusts the recording level to avoid distortion and amplify weak sounds, used mainly in portable cassette recorders. Also called "AGC," "ARL" or "ALC."

AUXILIARY LEVEL (AU)   On home audio equipment, used to denote line level, as opposed to mic or speaker level; also called "aux level."

AXIS   A straight line bisecting the area enclosed by a microphone's pickup pattern.

AZIMUTH   The angle (in one particular axis) of a tape head in relation to the recording tape, at the point where the tape passes over the head gap. (This angle should be exactly 90 degrees. Azimuth misalignment will result in loss of high frequencies. The head azimuth is adjustable to compensate for misalignment.)

BACK-CUE   To manually turn a phonograph record on a turntable platter counterclockwise while the stylus is in a groove, for purposes of exact cuing.

BAFFLE   A portable sound-absorbing structure, used to acoustically isolate any portion of a studio.

BALANCED CONNECTION   Any connection between two audio devices where three wires are used, such that two of the wires carry the desired signal and the third is the "ground." The wires are connected to a transformer or similar device on one end so that any unwanted signal that is induced into the circuit (such as hum from a power line) will cancel itself out.

BALUN   A device which matches an unbalanced line to a balanced line or vice versa; short for "balanced to unbalanced."

BANANA PLUG   A connector with a spring-metal tip, resembling a banana.

BAND   1. A specific range of frequencies. For example, the audio band extends from 16 Hz to 20,000 Hz. 2. A self-contained recording, usually among several, on one side of a phonograph record.

BANDWIDTH   A range of frequencies within a given band. For example, the bandwidth of the midrange frequencies of the audio band extends from 300 to 3,500 Hz.

BASS   See "low range."

BATTERY   A device which stores voltage (electric energy).

BED   Program material (usually music, sound effects or actualities) used as "background" for narration or other "foreground" sounds.

BIAS TONE   An inaudible, high-frequency tone (between 50 kHz and 150 kHz) placed on recording tape at the recording head of a tape machine, which minimizes distortion. (The level of bias current is adjustable in tape machines for different kinds of tape.)

BIDIRECTIONAL MICROPHONE   A microphone with a figure-8 pickup pattern, extending as two ovoid shapes in opposite directions like a dumbbell. Bidirectional mics have strong rejection to the sides perpendicular to the "dumbbell."

BINARY   In audio, a numerical system that uses only two digits, zero and one. Sequences of zeros and ones are used to represent the changing voltage of an audio signal, and thereby represent the original sound.

BINAURAL RECORDING   A system which attempts to record sounds as closely as possible to the way a pair of human ears would perceive them.

BIT   The word "bit" probably originated as an abbreviation for "binary digit."

BOARD   A device designed to mix and process the signals from the outputs of a number of other audio devices (mics, tape machines, turntables, etc.) for recording or broadcast purposes; also called "mixing board," "audio console," "mixing console."

BOOM   The extending arm of a microphone stand which allows the microphone to be moved in all directions.

BOOST   To increase (amplify) the level of a signal.

BREATHING   See "pumping."

BRIDGE   A sound element used to provide a gradual transition from one program segment to another, often denoting a change in time, space or mood.

BROADCAST LOOP   See "dedicated phone line."

BULK ERASER   See "degausser."

BUS   A circuit in a mixing board which carries signals from one or more inputs to any output or set of outputs, e.g., the "audition" channel of a broadcast board.

BUZZ Noise comprised of one or more multiples of 60 Hz, often induced from power current leaking into an audio circuit.

BYTE Some number of binary digits.

CABLE A wire, or several wires running parallel to each other, contained within an insulating sheath of plastic or cloth.

CABLE PAIR See "dedicated phone line."

CALIBRATE To bring the reading of any measuring device (e.g., a VU meter) into exact accordance with a fixed standard.

CANNON CONNECTOR A three-pin connector, most commonly used for connecting professional microphones and other balanced devices; also called "XLR connector."

CANS Headphones (slang).

CAPACITOR An electronic device used for accumulating and holding an electrical charge, consisting of two charged diaphragms, separated by a non-conductor; also called a "condenser."

CAPSTAN In a tape machine transport, a metal cylinder rotated by a motor which, in conjunction with the pinch roller, moves the tape past the heads at a precise operating speed.

CARDIOID "Heart-shaped," referring to the pickup pattern of the most common unidirectional microphones.

CART A continuous loop of ¼″ recording tape on a single spindle inside a plastic case; short for "cartridge."

CART MACHINE A tape machine that records and/or plays carts, and which can recue a cart to the beginning without rewinding.

CARTRIDGE 1. The device on a phonograph tone arm which houses the stylus and converts the movements of the stylus into analogous electrical signals; also "phono cartridge." 2. Cart.

CASSETTE A single length of recording tape permanently attached to the supply and take-up reels, housed in a small plastic container. (Standard audio cassettes use ⅛ inch wide recording tape, run at 1⅞ ips.)

CASSETTE MACHINE A tape machine that records and/or plays cassette tapes.

CASSETTE TABS Two small tabs on the back of cassette casings which engage a lever in the cassette machine that deactivates the record lock.

CD (compact disc)   A sound storage medium in which the sound is represented optically. During playback a laser scans the disc and is deflected by the irregularities that comprise the encoded sound.

CENTER FREQUENCY   The frequency in the middle of a frequency band being equalized.

CHANNEL   A path that an audio signal follows, such as the "audition" channel of a board, or the left and right channels of stereo devices.

CHASSIS   The metallic frame of a piece of audio equipment.

CHINA MARKER   See "grease pencil."

CHROMIUM DIOXIDE   A tape oxide formulation providing lower tape hiss than ferric oxide when used with machines on which the bias and equalization can be set specifically for it; abbreviated CrO_2.

CIRCUIT   The complete path of an electrical current.

CLIPPING   A kind of distortion caused by a device receiving a signal that is too loud for it. Clipping is characterized by a "crackling" sound. (For example, a mic pre-amp may be "clipped" when the mic picks up very loud sounds.)

CLIP WIRE   A wire with an alligator clip at each end, used for making grounding or temporary connections.

CLOSE MIKING   Placing a microphone within a few inches of the sound source.

COINCIDENT PAIR   See "crossed pair."

COLLAGE   A sound composition consisting of brief audio elements combined in such a way as to convey a desired message or image without the need for explanatory narration.

COLORATION   The artificial and usually undesirable alteration of reproduced sound resulting from poor frequency response.

COMPANDER   A combined compressor/expander.

COMPLEX SOUND   Sound made up of more than one frequency. (All natural sounds are complex sounds, as are buzz and hiss.)

COMPRESSION RATIO   The degree to which a compressor or limiter restricts the level of a signal which exceeds the threshold of compression.

COMPRESSION THRESHOLD   See "threshold of compression."

COMPRESSOR A device which narrows the dynamic range of a sound sequence (e.g., a symphony) by reducing the level of the louder parts so they are closer in level to the softer parts.

CONDENSER See "capacitor."

CONDENSER MICROPHONE A microphone from which electrical current is caused to flow by changes in the electrical relationship between the two plates of a capacitor (condenser), requiring either an internal battery or an external power supply.

CONDUCTOR Any material which allows an electrical current to flow through it.

CONE The part of a speaker which is vibrated to produce sound waves, the obverse of a dynamic microphone's diaphragm.

CONNECTOR A device used to link audio equipment.

CONSOLE See "board."

CONTINUITY Narration linking the elements of a program together.

CONTROL ROOM A room containing audio equipment set up to do production or recording work, or broadcasting. Control rooms are often, though not always, separate from the "studio" (room where the mics are set up).

COTTAGE LOAF A British term used to describe the pickup pattern of a hypercardioid microphone.

CrO$_2$ See "chromium dioxide."

CROSSED PAIR A stereo miking technique in which two cardioid microphones are placed at approximately right angles, in close proximity, or directly on top of one another.

CROSSFADE A mix in which one sound element is faded out as another is faded in, so that for a time both are heard.

CROSSOVER The frequency at which a signal is split to feed separate loudspeakers.

CROSSOVER NETWORK A device which splits a signal into high and low frequency components, sending the highs to one loudspeaker and the lows to another.

CROSSTALK Interference resulting from the "leaking" or "bleeding" of the signals from one audio circuit to another.

CUE   1. To listen to an audio element before it is broadcast or otherwise used. 2. The separate bus that most boards have for this purpose.

CUE SHEET   A written sheet or "flow chart" listing the sequence of sound elements to be mixed, kinds of segues, placement of effects, and so on.

CUING OUTPUT   An output on most broadcast consoles that leads to an amplifier and speaker (usually built into the console itself), allowing listening to incoming signals without sending them to the "main" or "audition" outputs.

CUT   1. A sudden transition from one sound element to another, done without fading. 2. See "band" (second definition).

CUT-AND-SPLICE EDITING   See "splice editing."

CYCLE   One complete vibration of a sound wave, or a single, complete alternation of an electrical current.

CYCLES PER SECOND   See "Hertz."

DASH   One of the many formats for recording audio digitally. Stands for "Digital Audio with Stationary Head."

DBX®   A type of noise reduction system.

DC   See "direct current."

DEAD ENVIRONMENT   One in which sound waves are absorbed rather than reflected (little echo or reverberation). Most studios are designed to be fairly dead.

DECAY   1. The time it takes for a sound to fade below the threshold of hearing. 2. The time it takes an echo or reverberation to fade below the threshold of hearing. 3. In compressor/limiters, release time.

DECIBEL   The unit of measurement by which the relative volumes of sounds are compared.

DECIBEL SCALE   A logarithmic scale used to compare the volumes of sounds, expressed in decibels. (Huge difference in volumes can be expressed by relatively small numbers, due to the logarithmic nature of the scale.)

DECODING   The process of expansion, in a compression/expansion noise reduction system.

DEDICATED PHONE LINE   A telephone line used specifically for carrying non-telephone audio signals, usually from a remote site to a broadcast station.

DEGAUSSER An electromagnet used to randomize existing magnetic fields or patterns; a *bulk eraser* randomizes ("erases") all the magnetic signals on a reel, cart or cassette of recording tape; a *head degausser* is a lower-powered, hand-held electromagnet used to demagnetize the metallic components of the tape path in a tape machine especially the heads.

DELAY 1. The interval of time between a sound and its first "echo." 2. An electronic device for creating an artificial, echo-like delay.

DENATURED ALCOHOL Ethyl alcohol mixed with a small amount of pyridine, methyl alcohol or other compounds, used to clean tape heads and other metal parts of the tape path. Available in drug stores.

DIAL-UP PHONE LINE A standard telephone line.

DIAPHRAGM A flexible membrane used to convert sound waves into electricity (as in a microphone), or electricity into sound waves (as in a loudspeaker).

DIGITAL AUDIO A system in which sound is represented by a series of numbers that correspond to the varying amplitudes of the sound's waveform.

DIGITAL AUDIO WORK STATION A set of computer hardware and software which allows sounds to be digitally recorded, processed, and mixed together.

DIGITAL TAPE TIMER Electronic timers that can give a "real-time" readout regardless of which tape speed is used. These are the most accurate tape timers.

DIRECT BOX A device, usually containing impedance matching transformers, which splits the output of a mic or electric instrument, sending the signal to two or more inputs (e.g., an electric guitar to a mixing board and the guitar amplifier).

DIRECT CURRENT The type of electrical current which flows in only one direction; as distinct from alternating current.

DIRECTIONAL CHARACTERISTICS See "pickup pattern."

DISTANT MIKING Placing a microphone a few feet or more from a sound source, so that more of the "room sound" will be heard.

DISTORTION Unwanted changes in sound quality caused by inaccurate electronic reproduction of sound. Most precisely, the creation of sounds by electronic processes (harmonics, etc.) which are related to the sound being produced.

DOCUMENTARY   A type of program that uses two or more audio elements (e.g., narration, interviews, music, actuality, drama, discussion, ambience, special effects) to tell a story.

DOLBY®   A noise reduction process.

DOLBY® TONE   A zero Vu level tone recorded at the beginning of reels of tape containing Dolby® encoded programs, to insure that the level of the signal sent through the Dolby® unit during decoding is identical to the level set through the unit during encoding.

DOUBLE MIKING   Using two microphones for each sound source to allow two separate mixes. For example, when a concert is broadcast, one set of mics may be set up for the live audience, and one set of mics for the radio broadcast.

DROPOUT   Loss of signal when recording on tape, caused by flaws in the oxide coating or debris covering a portion of the oxide coating.

DUB   1. (*verb*) To make a copy of a tape recording. 2. (*noun*) A copy of a tape recording.

DUCT TAPE   An extra-strong, extra-adhesive, easily-torn cloth tape, usually about two inches wide; the sound person's friend. Also called "gray tape," "silver tape," or "gaffer's tape."

DURATION   The length (time) of a sound.

DYNAMIC MICROPHONE   A microphone having a thin diaphragm attached to a coil of wire mounted in the field of a permanent magnet. (Sound waves striking the microphone cause the diaphragm to vibrate, moving the coil back and forth through the magnetic field, which generates the electrical signal.)

DYNAMIC RANGE   The difference in volume between the quietest sound and loudest sound in any sound sequence, e.g., a symphony.

DYNAMICS   The variation in the volume of sound.

DYNAMIC SPEAKER   The most common type of loudspeaker, operating on principles similar to a dynamic mic, but in "reverse."

ECHO   The delayed, audible repetition of a sound.

EDIT   Remove or rearrange segments of a recorded tape.

EDITING BLOCK   See "splicing block."

EIA REEL   A 10½-inch tape reel with a small hole in the center.

ELECTRET CONDENSER MICROPHONE A type of condenser microphone whose element requires no power supply in order to operate.

ELECTROMAGNET A temporary magnet, formed by electrical current flowing through a coil of wire wrapped around a steel or iron core.

ELECTRONIC EDITING Removing or rearranging segments of a tape recording by selectively dubbing segments from one tape machine to another.

ELECTRONICS See "tape machine electronics."

ELECTROSTATIC SPEAKER A less common type of loudspeaker operating on principles similar to those of a condenser microphone (utilizing a "giant capacitor"), but in "reverse."

ELEMENT 1. The part of a microphone which converts sound to an electrical analog, the part of speaker that converts electricity to sound, or the part of a tape head which converts electricity to a magnetic analog or vice versa. 2. Any portion of an audio program (music, continuity, actualities, effects, etc.).

ELLIPTICAL STYLUS A type of stylus seldom used in audio production because it cannot be used in back-cuing.

ENCODING The process of compression, in a compression/expansion noise reduction system.

EQUALIZATION The process of amplifying or attenuating certain frequencies within a specific sound in relation to the other frequencies within that same sound; also, "EQ."

EQUALIZED PHONE LINE A telephone line which has been equalized so that it has flat frequency response over a wide range of frequencies.

EQUALIZER A device used for equalization.

ERASE To randomize magnetic signals of recording tape by exposing it to a strong, random magnetic field.

ERASE HEAD The component of a tape machine that randomizes (erases) the patterned magnetic signals on a tape recording, in preparation for recording.

EXOTIC MONITOR FEED A mix sent through a separate output bus which is different from the mix being sent out the main output bus; for example, a feed sent to musicians performing in a studio.

EXPANDER A device that widens the dynamic range of a sound sequence.

FADE   The gradual increase or decrease in volume of any audio element. (A fade-in is an increase in volume from zero to the desired level and a fade-out is a decrease from the existing level to zero.)

F-1   A format for recording sounds digitally, which uses a video tape recorder, and a separate unit which does the conversion from analog to digital and back again.

FADER   A volume pot that slides up and down, as opposed to a rotating knob.

FAST WOUND   Describes tape that has been wound in the "fast-forward" or "rewind" modes.

FCC   Federal Communications Commission.

FEATURE   A short documentary-style production.

FeCr   See "ferro-chromium."

FEED   1. Transmission of an audio signal from one location to another, or from one device to another—for example, a phone line signal is "fed" to an equalizer. 2. The signal thus transmitted.

FEEDBACK   The result of an output signal from an audio device being fed back into its own input; when audible, this potentially damaging situation is characterized by a "howling" or "ringing" sound.

FEEDBACK (Acoustic)   A form of feedback in which the output of a mic is reproduced through a speaker which is picked up by the same mic, and so on.

FEED TECHNIQUE   A means of broadcasting a remote event where the PA mix is "fed" to the radio station for broadcast through a spare output bus on the PA board.

Fe$_2$O   See "ferric oxide."

FERRIC OXIDE   The most commonly used recording tape oxide; abbreviated "Fe$_2$O."

FERRO-CHROMIUM   A recording tape oxide; abbreviated "FeCr."

FIELD PATTERN   See "polar pattern."

15 kHz PHONE LINE   A high-quality, equalized phone line with a flat or nearly flat frequency response up to 15 kHz.

FIGURE 8 MIC   See "bidirectional microphone."

FILTER   1. A type of equalizer used for reducing the level of some specific band of frequencies. 2. To equalize, especially to attenuate, a specific frequency or frequencies.

5 kHz PHONE LINE   An equalized telephone line with a flat response up to 5 kHz.

FLANGE   One of the "sides of a tape reel. See also "hub."

FLANGING   Phase cancellation characterized by a "swishing" sound. Also called "comb filtering."

FLAT RESPONSE   Accurate reproduction by an audio device of all of the frequencies fed into it, without amplifying or attenuating any group of frequencies within the signal.

FLUTTER   A fast and regular variation in the speed of the transport of a tape machine or turntable, resulting in a "fluttering" sound.

FOLDBACK   An exotic monitor feed where each performer in a recording session is provided with a special mix, as opposed to the mix being recorded for broadcast.

FREQUENCY   The rate of vibration of a sound wave or an electrical signal measured in Hertz (cycles per second).

FREQUENCY RESPONSE   The degree to which an audio device is capable of reproducing all of the frequencies fed into it without amplifying or attenuating a frequency or group of frequencies within the signal.

FULL-TRACK   A track configuration in which a single, mono signal is recorded across nearly the entire width of the recording tape; "one-track."

FUNDAMENTAL VIBRATION   The lowest frequency in a complex vibration.

FUSE   A device containing a piece of metal or wire with a low melting point, put into an electrical circuit, which melts ("fuses") when too high a level of current is fed into the circuit, thus breaking the circuit and preventing damage to other devices.

FX   A common abbreviation for "sound effects."

GAFFER'S TAPE   See "duct tape."

GAIN   1. Any change in volume. 2. The amount of amplification in a given device or system, expressed in decibels.

GAIN STRUCTURE   Any system within which signals change in amplitude, e.g., a public address system.

GAP   The tiny distance between the two poles of a magnetic tape head.

"GETTING A LEVEL"   Sending a representative sample of program material to a device to adjust the appropriate volume controls or to obtain proper mic placement, prior to recording or broadcast.

GLITCH   A "smudge" of sound on an otherwise quiet portion of tape.

GOODNIGHTING THE LINE   Calling the telephone company to have a phone line for a remote broadcast disconnected.

GOOSENECK   A type of microphone stand, or attachment for a mike stand, usually flexible, which allows for movable mike positioning.

GRAPHIC EQUALIZER   A type of equalizer having discrete linear faders, arranged side by side, used to control specific bands of frequencies.

GREASE PENCIL   A soft, waxy pencil used to mark the back of recording tape during splice editing; also called "wax pencil" or "china marker."

GROUND   1. (*noun*) In an electrical system, the point of lowest potential. (An electrical current flows from a point of high potential to a point of low potential. The Earth itself is the ideal ground, because it has zero potential.) 2. (*noun*) Ground wire. 3. (*verb*) To connect to a ground wire.

GROUND LOOP   An undesirable condition caused by improper grounding between audio devices, which can result in a strong hum or buzz.

GROUND WIRE   A conductor which makes an electrical connection to a ground, often the Earth itself.

GUARD BAND   In multi-track (two or more) track configurations, the small space between one track and the next, where there are no recorded signals. This serves to reduce "crosstalk" between the tracks.

HALF-TRACK   A track configuration in which the signal is recorded on nearly half of the width of the recording tape. (In "half-track stereo"—two track—two signals are placed on the tape, each occupying a little less than half the width.)

HARD WIRING   Permanent connections made by soldering, as opposed to those using plugs and jacks.

HARMONICS   Multiples of a fundamental frequency.

HEAD   1. The component of a tape recorder, over which the tape passes, that either erases any signals present on the tape, records new signals on the tape, or reproduces existing signals from the tape. 2. The beginning of a recorded program.

HEADS IN   See "tails out."

HEADS OUT   (A tape) wound so the beginning ("head") of a recorded program is outermost on the reel, thus eliminating the necessity of rewinding it before playing.

HEADPHONES   Very small speakers in a headset and worn against the ears.

HEAD ROOM   Usually, the amount of amplification possible *before* distortion but *after* the signal being processed by a device has already registered zero VU.

HERTZ   Cycles per second, the unit of measurement for frequency.

HIGH CUT FILTER   A type of equalizer in which all the high frequencies above a pre-set limit are attenuated.

HIGH FREQUENCY   See "high range."

HIGH LEVEL INPUT   See "line level."

HIGH OUTPUT TAPE   Audio recording tape with an oxide formulation designed to allow a stronger (louder) signal before distortion than "standard output tape."

HIGH RANGE (HIGHS)   Any frequency above approximately 3,000 Hz.

HISS   A kind of complex, high-frequency noise inherent in recording tape and audio amplification; the most common noise problem in recording work.

HOLDFAST   The tightening clamp on a microphone stand.

HUB   The part of a tape reel around which the tape winds, as distinguished from the flanges (sides) of the reel, and the spindle hole (center) of the reel.

HUM   Audible noise caused by 60 Hz alternating current leaking into an audio circuit, often caused by broken or improperly-wired cables.

HYPERCARDIOID   A specific kind of unidirectional microphone pickup pattern, possessing extreme rejection to sounds coming all directions except that in which it is pointed.

IMPEDANCE   The total resistance to an alternating current presented by a given circuit.

IMPEDANCE MATCHING TRANSFORMER   A device used to artificially match the impedances of two pieces of audio equipment.

INCHES PER SECOND The unit of measurement for recording speed.

INDUCTION An electrical phenomenon in which a signal in one set of wires causes an identical signal to flow in an adjacent set of wires, because of the magnetic field generated by the original signal. (This is the most common reason that a broken or miswired cable can cause hum or buzz. The hum or buzz is induced into the cable from the AC power line. A properly-wired cable is designed to prevent this kind of induction.)

IN-KIND EXPENSE The cost of materials, facilities, or labor on a production (or other project) that are donated to the project. For instance, if the going rate for studio rental is $50/hour, but the studio has been used for three hours without payment, the studio time can be considered an in-kind expense of $150.

INPUT 1. In an audio device, the place (both the connector and the circuit) into which an incoming signal is fed. 2. The incoming signal being sent to the recording head, *before* it is put on tape.

INTENSITY The amplitude of a sound or signal.

INTERFACE To connect two or more devices.

INTRO Introduction (beginning) of a program; theme music, title, etc.

IPS Inches per second.

JACK A socket or receptacle connector, which mates with a plug.

JACK FIELD See "patch bay."

k Abbreviation for "kilo-."

kHz KiloHertz, or thousand Hertz.

KILO- One thousand (combining form); 1k = 1,000.

LAVALIER MICROPHONE A small omni-directional microphone which can be suspended from a cord worn around the neck or clipped onto clothing; named for a courtesan of Louis XIV(!), and sometimes called a "lapel mic."

LEADER A colored (sometimes clear) plastic or paper tape which has the same dimensions as audio tape, but has no magnetic oxide coating.

LEVEL The volume or intensity of a sound or signal.

LEVEL MATCHING The science of connecting the correct level output with the correct level input.

LIFTING   A type of patch bay connection in which the normalled connection is broken ("lifted") when a patch is thrown.

LIMITER   A type of compressor with a very high compression ratio and usually having fast attack and release times.

LINE   Any circuit.

LINE INPUT   An input designed to receive signals at line level.

LINE LEVEL   One of the three signal levels of audio devices, greater than mic level and less than speaker level; the level of signal with which most electronic audio circuits operate.

LIVE   1. A program broadcast as it is being produced (as distinct from being recorded for later broadcast). 2. (*of an acoustical environment*) Tending to reflect sounds rather than absorb them. 3. A microphone that is "on" or "up."

LOG   1. A table of contents of any recorded program, or program material. 2. Program log.

LOOP   A piece of tape or film with a recording on it, spliced into a loop so that it can be played continuously.

LOUDNESS   Subjective perception of the intensity or volume of a sound.

LOUDSPEAKER   A device which converts an electrical signal into an audible sound.

LOW CUT FILTER   One of the simplest kinds of equalizers that, when activated, completely filters out a fixed range of low frequencies.

LOW FREQUENCY   See "low range."

LOW LEVEL INPUT   See "mic level."

LOW RANGE (LOWS)   Any frequency below approximately 400 Hertz.

m   Abbreviation for "mega-."

MASTER   An original recording, from which copies (dubs) are made; also called "mother."

MECHANICAL TAPE TIMER   A tape timer that generally only reads real time at one speed, usually 7½ ips. A mechanical timer is less accurate than a digital timer.

MEGA-   Million (combining form); $1m = 1,000,000$.

MEGAHERTZ   Million Hertz.

METER-AND-OUTPUT SWITCH   The switch on the front panel of a tape machine's electronics which allows the choice of metering and monitoring the incoming, "INPUT" signal (before it is put on tape), or the "PLAYBACK" signal (from the tape itself).

MIC   Abbreviation for "microphone."

MICROPHONE   A device capable of transforming the air-pressure wave of sound into analogous changes in electrical currents (voltage), used in recording or transmitting sound.

MIDI   Stands for "Musical Instrument Digital Interface." A system for interconnecting sevral electronic musical instruments, like synthesizers, so that each can be controlled by the others.

MIDRANGE (MIDS)   Any frequency between approximately 400 and 3,000 Hertz.

MIC SPLITTING   A miking technique in which the signals from microphones on a stage are "split" and sent to the inputs of two different boards, so that two different mixes (for instance, broadcast and PA) can be obtained using only one set of mics.

MIC LEVEL   Lowest of the three signal levels of audio devices. (A mic level signal is pre-amplified to line level before being processed further.)

MIL   One thousandth of an inch. (Not to be confused with "millimeter," which is a thousandth of a meter.) Audio recording tape comes in the standard thickness of 1½ mil, 1 mil, and ½ mil.

MINI CONNECTOR   A type of plug or jack, often used with cassette machines.

MICROPHONE CONNECTOR   See "mini connector."

MIX   1. (*verb*) To combine two or more audio signals (inputs) into one audio signal. 2. (*noun*) The combination of two or more audio signals.

MIXER   See "board."

MIXING BOARD   See "board."

MIXING CONSOLE   See "board."

MODULE   The basic building block of a recording studio or sound reinforcement mixing console. A module usually includes a principal fader, secondary fader, assignment switches, panning knobs, equalizer, and auxilliary sends. It is sometimes called a "slice" because it is usually long and narrow, like each slice of a loaf of bread when the loaf is viewed from above, along one of its long sides.

MONAURAL   See "mono."

MONITOR   1. (*verb*) To listen to. 2. (*noun*) A loudspeaker, headphone, etc.

MONO   Pertaining to a sound reproduction system that produces a single output signal from one or more input signals; short for "monaural" or "monophonic."

MONOPHONIC   See "mono."

MONTAGE   A layering of superimposition of disparate sound elements conveying a single sound image.

MOTHER   See "master."

MOVING COIL MICROPHONE   See "dynamic microphone."

MS MIKING TECHNIQUE   Mid-side miking, a technique involving a special microphone with two different pickup elements inside it, or two separate but closely-placed microphones. One has a figure-eight pattern, and is usually arranged so that the lobes of the "8" are positioned at a ninety degree angle to the direction of the sound source. The other element is usually cardioid, and is pointed directly at the sound source. Combining the two signals results in a stereo signal.

MULTI-CHANNEL BOARD   A mixing board with a main output bus having more than two channels, usually between four and thirty-two, each of which can be assigned to a different input of a multi-track tape machine.

MULTI-MIKING   Close miking a sound event consisting of more than one sound source.

MULTI-TRACK TAPE RECORDER   A tape recorder that is capable of recording more than two separate channels (tracks) at once, with one recording element for each track. (Multi-track tape recorders allow recordings that are made with more than two inputs to be remixed any number of times.)

MUTE   To silence, as a microphone or loudspeaker.

MUTING   A standard wiring procedure in studios which automatically silences the loudspeaker monitors when a mic pot is opened, thus avoiding feedback.

MYLAR   A plastic material used as a recording tape backing, similar to polyester.

NAB   National Association of Broadcasters.

NAB ADAPTER   An adapter which is used with a NAB reel to allow it to fit over a regular spindle.

NAB REEL   A type of 10½" tape reel with an extra-wide center hole.

NEEDLE   See "stylus."

NICAD   See "nickel cadmium."

NICKEL CADMIUM   A type of battery which is capable of being recharged.

NOISE   Any undesirable sound in a broadcast or recording, especially hiss, hum, buzz RF, and unwanted ambience.

NOISE REDUCTION DEVICE   An electronic system utilizing compression, expansion and equalization to avoid some of the noise inherent in audio tape and circuitry.

NON-LIFTING   A type of patch bay connection in which the normalled connection is not broken (lifted) when a patch is thrown.

NON-REAL-TIME   In a production, involving a final studio mix of all the sound elements to be used in a program; as distinct from a "real-time" production of a "live" event.

NORMALLED CONNECTION   A standard wiring procedure for patch bays, such that connections between certain devices exist without the necessity of throwing a patch.

NRU   See "noise reduction device."

OFF-AXIS   In reference to sound waves, originating from a point outside the pickup pattern of a microphone.

OHM   The unit of measurement for electrical resistance; symbolized by the Greek letter "Ω".

OMNI-   An omnidirectional microphone.

OMNIDIRECTIONAL   The pickup pattern of a microphone designed to be equally sensitive to sound coming from any direction. (No commonly used microphone is omnidirectional in terms of high frequency response. Even omni mics will not respond evenly to the frequencies above 5,000 Hz in any sound originating "behind" the mic.)

ON-AXIS   In reference to sound waves, originating from a point well inside the pickup pattern of a microphone.

OPEN REEL   A tape machine which uses tape that isn't permanently housed in a cartridge or cassette; also called "reel-to-reel."

OPERATOR   The person using an audio device.

OSCILLATOR   An electronic device which produces an alternating current at a particular frequency; in particular, an audio oscillator can generate pure tones at any frequency within the audio range.

OSCILLOSCOPE   An electronic device that uses a cathode ray tube (similar to a television picture tube) to give a visual representation of electrical signals.

OUTPUT   1. In an audio device, the place (both the connector and the circuit) from which a signal is sent to another device. 2. The outgoing signal being sent from one device to another.

OUTRO   The very end of a program, including final theme music, credits, etc.

OVERDUB   To record a new track or tracks in synchronization with a previously-recorded track or tracks.

OVERLOADING   See "overmodulating."

OVERMODULATING   Sending a signal into a circuit or device which is at too high a level to be processed properly, usually resulting in distortion (see also "clipping").

OXIDE   The magnetizable particles coating almost all recording tape, which form the magnetic patterns that store the analog signals.

PA SYSTEM   See "public address system."

PACK   The degree of evenness and compactness with which any particular reel of tape winds on a reel. (A "good pack" is one that is completely smooth and even, with no "ripples" or tape edges sticking out. The fast-wind modes do not give a good pack; the "PLAY" mode should.)

PAD   A resistor device used to attenuate an electrical signal. (Pads are often used to prevent the output of a mic from overloading its pre-amp.)

PAN   A stereo mixing effect, made by moving a sound to one channel from the other using a pan pot, giving the illusion of motion.

PAN POT   The control that determines to which output channel an input signal is sent, or assigned; short for "panoramic potentiometer." (See also "potentiometer.")

PARAMETRIC EQUALIZER A type of equalizer allowing complete and variable control over all three equalization parameters (*amount* of boost or attenuation, *bandwidth* being boosted or attenuated, and the *center frequency* of each band being boosted or attenuated.)

PATCH 1. (*verb*) To connect by means of a patch bay and patchcords. 2. (*noun*) A connection thus made.

PATCH BAY A centralized bank of jacks, each of which is hard-wired to a cable leading to the input or output of each piece of equipment in a production room or studio, used to simplify the connecting of the devices; also called "patch panel" or "jack field."

PATCH CABLE See "patchcord."

PATCHCORD A short cable with a plug at each end, used to make connections between input and output jacks located in a patch bay.

PATCH PANEL See "patch bay."

PATTERN See "pickup pattern."

PD Stands for "Professional Digital." A format for recording sounds digitally.

PEAK 1. The loudest part of a sound sequence; or, any portion of particularly high volume. 2. (*verb*) To reach highest volume. 3. (*verb*) To light up the peak flasher.

PEAK FLASHER The small light, usually red, situated near a meter on a tape machine, which flashes to indicate peaks in the signal which the meter needle may not be quick enough to reflect.

PEAK METER See "peak program meter."

PEAK PROGRAM METER A meter which indicates the peaks in the program material, rather than averaging the volume as a VU meter does.

PHANTOM POWERING A method of powering condenser mics remotely, in which the two audio carrying wires have the same DC voltage. Phantom powering does not affect the operation of dynamic microphones.

PHASE The degree of synchronicity between two vibrating objects, electrical currents or sound waves. (Two signals are "in phase" when their cycles are exactly synchronous.)

PHASE CANCELLATION The phenomenon occurring when two identical signals are combined, very slightly out of synchronicity, causing loss of some frequencies.

PHONE CONNECTOR   A type of plug or jack commonly used with audio devices, which comes in mono (two-conductor or "tip-sleeve") and stereo (three-conductor, to "tip-ring-sleeve") varieties. Phone connectors are also called "quarter-inch connectors." Not to be confused with phono (RCA) connectors.

PHONE COUPLING DEVICE   A device enabling a dial-up phone line to be connected to audio equipment, preventing damage to the equipment from any direct current present in the phone line.

PHONE LINES   The wires used to transmit telephone signals.

PHONO CARTRIDGE   See "cartridge."

PHONO CONNECTOR   See "RCA connector."

PICKUP   Any device that changes mechanical vibration, sound, or alternating magnetic fields into electrical signals.

PICKUP ARM   See "tone arm."

PICKUP PATTERN   The area from within which a sound source must originate in order for a microphone to "pick it up" (reproduce it) with good frequency response.

PINCH ROLLER   The rubber wheel that presses the recording tape against the capstan of a tape machine.

PITCH   The fundamental frequency of a sound.

PLAY   See "playback."

PLAYBACK HEAD   The component of a tape machine that converts the magnetic signals stored on recording tape into electrical signals; also called "reproduce head."

PLAYBACK LEVEL   The volume of the signal being sent to the outputs of a tape machine.

PLOSIVE   Referring to the short burst of air from the mouth that is produced when a consonant such as "p," "t," or "b" is spoken. Plosive sounds may cause "popping" if spoken into a microphone from too close a distance.

PLUG   The "male" connector designed to mate with a jack ("female" connector).

POLAR PATTERN   A diagram representing a microphone's sensitivity to sounds coming from different directions.

POLYESTER   A plastic material used as recording tape backing.

POP FILTER   A device designed to shield a microphone's element from popping or wind, e.g., a foam windscreen.

POPPING   The undesirable sound made by the short bursts of air coming from the mouth when plosive consonants are spoken.

POST-PRODUCTION   Processing of program material that takes place after the initial recording. Post-production includes such functions as editing, mixing, and equalizing.

POT   See "potentiometer."

POTENTIOMETER   A resistance device which can vary the amount of voltage in a circuit, and thus acts as a volume control.

POWER   The electrical current available from a wall socket.

POWER AMPLIFIER   A device which boosts line level electrical signals to speaker level.

PPM   See "peak program meter."

PRE-AMPLIFIER   A device which boosts electrical signals from mic level to line level.

PRESENCE   The quality in a recording of a voice or instrument which gives the impression of the sound source being close to the listener; this is sometimes enhanced by boosting certain frequencies within the 2 kHz to 8 kHz range.

PRINT-THROUGH   The undesirable transfer of magnetic signals from one layer of recording tape wound on a reel to the layer immediately above or below it, causing an "echo" or "pre-echo" effect in playback.

PRODUCER   The person in charge of putting together a program.

PRODUCTION   The putting together of a program, requiring such operations as recording, editing, and mixing.

PROGRAM   1. A complete broadcast presentation. 2. Program channel.

PROGRAM CHANNEL   The main output of a mixing board.

PROGRAM LOG   The written record of the material broadcast every day on a radio station, item by item.

PROGRAM OUTPUT   See "program channel."

PROXIMITY EFFECT The tendency of a microphone, particularly cardioid mics, to boost the bass frequencies of sound sources placed very close to (within a few inches of) the microphone.

PUBLIC ADDRESS SYSTEM A series of audio components which serve to amplify sound (of musicians or politicians, for example) so that it may be heard by a large number of people; also called a "sound reinforcement system" or PA. (The simplest public address system consists of a microphone, a pre-amplifier, a power amplifier, a loudspeaker, and cables connecting these devices in sequence.)

PCM (Pulse Code Modulation) A system for representating sound in which a series of numbers, which are actually pulses, stand for the amplitudes of the sound's waveforms.

PUMPING An undesirable "whooshing" sound which sometimes occurs while using a compressor with a fast release time. If there is a quick succession of high-level peaks followed by short silences, the change in level of the background hiss (as the output level of the compressor rises sharply) will be audible; also called "breathing."

PURE TONE A sound, electronically generated, containing only one frequency.

QUARTER-INCH CONNECTOR See "phone connector."

QUARTER-TRACK A track configuration in which a signal is recorded on a track that is slightly less than one-quarter the width of the tape, and which has the capability of recording a stereo (two-channel) signal in both directions on a single tape. (This should not be confused with "four-track," which is a multi-track configuration allowing *four* tracks of signal to be recorded *simultaneously*, in one direction.)

RACK A cabinet, usually metal, designed to hold professional audio equipment (tape machines, equalizers, etc.) in a working studio set-up; usually 19″ wide.

RADIATION The process by which energy is transmitted, or propagated, through space.

RADIO Communication by electromagnetic waves radiated through space.

RADIO FREQUENCY Any frequency between the audio range and the infrared light portion of the spectrum (approximately 15 kHz to 10,000,000 mHz), specifically any radio signal; abbreviated "RF."

RADIO FREQUENCY SHOT Sending program material from one place to another by means of a remote pickup unit; commonly abbreviated as "RF shot."

RCA CONNECTOR   A type of plug or jack, commonly used in audio equipment and especially in home stereo equipment; also called "phono connector." (Since an RCA connector is always mono, two of them must be used to carry a stereo signal.)

RDAT (Recording Digital Audio Tape)   A system for storing audio in digital (PCM) form on small cassettes. These recorders are suitable for "consumer" and portable applications.

R-DAT   Stands for "Rotating head Digital Audio Taperecorder." A system for recording sounds digitally which uses a rotating head similar to some video tape recorders.

REAL-TIME   Referring to a production involving an event that is being broadcast "live" or an event whose nature (an audience, for example) does not allow "retakes," as distinct from a non-real-time studio production.

RECORD   1. (*noun*) A phonograph record. 2. (*verb*) To store an audio signal.

RECORDING   1. (*noun*) A tape recording. 2. (*verb*) Storing signals.

RECORDING HEAD   The component of a tape machine which converts an electrical audio signal into a pattern of magnetic signals on recording tape.

RECORDING LEVEL   The volume of the incoming signal being sent to the recording head, before it is put on tape.

RECORDING TAPE   A magnetizable oxide coating on a plastic backing, used to store information by means of magnetic analog signals.

RECORD LOCK   A feature of many cassette tape recorders which, when activated, prevents the machine from operating in the record mode. When a cassette is inserted into the machine, two small "tabs" on the "back" of the cassette casing engage a lever in the machine which deactivates the Record Lock and allows the machine to record.

REEL   A large, flat spool on which recording tape is wound; common audio tape reel sizes are 5", 7" and 10½".

REEL MOTOR   An electric motor which turns the spindle of a tape machine and helps move the tape across the heads; part of the tape transport system.

REEL-TO-REEL   See "open reel."

RELEASE TIME   The length of time it takes for a compressor to allow its output signal to return to the pre-compression level.

REMOTE Any recording or broadcast done outside of a radio station, TV station, or production center.

REMOTE PICKUP UNIT A special portable radio transmitter which is used to send a signal from a remote site back to a special, compatible receiver at the radio station for recording or broadcast. Commonly referred to as an RPU.

REPRODUCE See "playback."

REPRODUCE HEAD See "playback head."

RESISTANCE Opposition to the flow of electricity; symbolized "R."

REVERBERATION (REVERB) A reflected sound which is "repeated" more than once.

RF See "radio frequency."

RF SHOT See "radio frequency shot."

RIBBON MICROPHONE A microphone similar in operation to a dynamic microphone, but with a strip of metallic ribbon acting as both the diaphragm and the moving conductor within the magnetic field.

RIDE THE GAIN To continuously monitor the level of a signal being recorded or reproduced, and adjust it as necessary.

ROLL-OFF Attenuation, used especially with reference to equalization.

ROOM TONE A recording of the ambience of an environment in which a recording of some sound event (for example, an interview) has just been made, used to "mask" artificial lapses in sound which may be necessitated by later editing.

RPU See "remote pickup unit."

SAMPLE To "sample" a sound means essentially the same thing as "to record" a sound. Some digital devices such as synthesizers and digital audio work stations can sample (record) a sound, holding it in electronic memory rather than recording it on tape or disc. This sound can be processed while in this electronic storage, then stored (recorded) on tape, disk, or other format later.

SATURATION A "muddying" distortion resulting from recording a signal at too great a volume.

SCHEMATIC DIAGRAM A symbolic representation of the electrical circuits and components of an electronic device or system.

SCRAPE FLUTTER   A distortion caused by audio tape vibrating as it passes over the surface of the tape heads, producing a "squealing" sound which varies with the signal. Scrape flutter may occur with cheap, poorly lubricated tape.

SEGUE   A transition between any two foreground elements or program segments, made by using a fade, a crossfade, or a cut.

SELECTIVE SYNCHRONIZATION   The optional capability of a three-head tape machine to reproduce a previously-recorded track at the recording head rather than the usual playback head, thus eliminating the delay between the "INPUT" and "PLAYBACK" signals and permitting the synchronous recording of new tracks (overdubbing); usually called "sync."

SHOCK-MOUNT   A device that physically isolates a microphone from any mechanical vibrations transmitted through the microphone stand which could produce low frequency noise; often, some type of elastic material from which the microphone is suspended.

SHOTGUN MICROPHONE   An extremely unidirectional microphone, used especially often in television and film work.

SIBILANCE   High frequency "s" and "ch" sounds in speech, sometimes reduced by placing the microphone to one side of the speaker's mouth.

SIGNAL   An electrical, magnetic, or optical representation of a sound.

SIGNAL-TO-NOISE RATIO   The difference in volume between the average level of the signal in a recording or broadcast, and the average level of noise being recorded or broadcast, expressed in decibels. ("Signal," by definition, is the *desired* information. A signal-to-noise ratio of over 50 decibels is considered adequate in many instances; 40 decibels or lower is poor.)

SLATING   Identifying individual segments of a recording by also recording a voice description on the tape immediately before the segment itself.

SLIDE POT (SLIDER)   See "fader."

SNAKE   A multi-wire cable which can carry the signals from many microphones, each on its own pair of wires.

SOUND   Vibrations which can be heard by the human ear, occurring in the audio range of frequencies between 16 Hz and 20,000 kHz.

SOUND CHECK   A final, "dress rehearsal" run-through of any PA, recording or broadcasting set-up for an event, in order to make sure that all the equipment is working correctly, to obtain a proper mix, and to iron out any last-minute problems before a performance begins.

SOUND REINFORCEMENT   See "public address system."

SOUND WAVE   The energy from an object vibrating at an audible rate, surging (like an ocean wave) through some elastic medium—such as air.

SOURCE   See "input."

SPEAKER   A device which changes electrical energy into sound.

SPEAKER LEVEL   The strongest of the three signal levels in audio devices; the output of a power amplifier is at speaker level.

SPEAKERPHONE   A device which connects a telephone to a board or tape recorder so that both ends of a conversation can be recorded; it has a volume control and is connected to a loudspeaker which allows more than one person to hear the person on the "other end."

SPEAKER SYSTEM   Any loudspeaker containing more than one cone.

SPHERICAL STYLUS   The kind of phonograph stylus used in radio work, which can be moved back and forth in the record groove for cuing purposes.

SPINDLE   The shaft on which a phonograph record or a reel of tape revolves.

SPINDLE HOLE   The hole in the center of a phonograph record or tape reel that fits over the spindle.

SPLICE   1. (*verb*) To physically attach two pieces of recording tape by butting their ends together and joining them with a piece of adhesive tape. 2. (*noun*) A tape join that is made by splicing.

SPLICE EDITING   Removing or rearranging segments of a program by physically cutting and splicing the tape on which it is recorded; also called "cut-and-splicing editing."

SPLICING BLOCK   A metal block which holds recording tape while it is being cut and spliced, guiding the angle of the razor blade and ensuring the proper fit between the ends of the tape.

SPLICING TAPE   A special kind of adhesive tape used for splicing.

SPLIT MIKING   See "mic splitting."

SPLITTER BOX   A device which splits the signals from one or more microphones and sends them to two or more places by means of snakes; also called a "stage box."

Spot Announcement A short radio announcement (station ID, special program promo, PSA, etc.), often pre-produced and taped; usually called simply "spot."

Squid A specialized set of cables, each having a cannon connector on one end, and all leading to a single connector on the other.

Stage Box See "splitter box."

Stage Monitor A speaker through which performers on stage are able to hear themselves; it usually involves a different mix of sound than on the PA speakers.

Standard Output Tape "Ordinary" audio tape, which cannot record as high a level of signal as "high output" tape.

Stereo The aspect of an audio program which allows it to be reproduced through two or more speakers such that the sound from one speaker is different in some way from that of the others. Often refers to the reproduction of left/right perspective.

Stereo Miking using two or more microphones to obtain signals containing different information from the same sound event, which are mixed into the two channels of a stereo recording; when the tape is replayed, a sound "perspective," is achieved.

Stereophonic See "stereo."

Studio A room in which recording is done.

Stylus The "needle" of a phonograph pickup arm, which rides in the grooves of a phonograph record, transmitting the vibrations to the cartridge in which it is housed.

Sum 1. (*verb*) To combine the outputs of all the microphones in a multi-miking set-up into a mono signal, one at a time, to check for level loss or tone discoloration which could indicate phase problems. 2. (*noun*) Another name for the main output bus of a board.

Supply Reel The reel from which cassette or open-reel recording tape unwinds as it plays or records. The supply reel is also called the "feed reel," as opposed to the "pickup reel."

Sync See "selective synchronization."

Tail The end of a recorded program.

Tails In Describes a tape that has been wound so that the end of the recorded program is innermost on the reel. See "heads out."

TAILS OUT Referring to a tape wound so the end ("tail") of a recorded program is outermost on the reel, thus making it necessary to rewind it before playing.

TAKE-UP REEL The reel onto which cassette or open-reel recording tape winds as it plays or records.

TALENT Those people heard "on the air" in a radio program (announcers, actors, musicians, guests and hosts.)

TALKBACK System for communication between studio and control room.

TAPE See "recording tape."

TAPE ECHO A delay produced by feeding the output of a tape recorder's playback head into the recorder's input during recording, which gives an artificial echo-like effect.

TAPE LOOP A length of tape spliced to form a continuous loop. Used in cartridge machines and for special repeating sound effects.

TAPE MACHINE Any device designed to record or playback signals on recording tape.

TAPE MACHINE ELECTRONICS The part of a tape machine which processes the audio signal during recording and playback.

TAPE RECORDER A tape machine which is able to record signals on recording tape.

TAPE RECORDING Electrical signals stored by means of magnetic patterns on recording tape.

TAPE TIMER Electronic or mechanical counter which measures length and/or time of any taped program or program segment as it is playing; the most useful tape timers can also time a tape in fast-wind modes.

TECHNICIAN A person who operates or maintains equipment.

TELEPHONE SET A typical telephone.

TENSIONERS The movable arms in the tape transport path which help maintain a constant and even tension on the tape as it winds and unwinds.

THREE-HEAD TAPE RECORDER A tape recorder with separate erase, recording and playback heads.

THREE-PIN CONNECTOR See "cannon connector."

THREE-WAY SPEAKER SYSTEM   One in which sound is reproduced by three separate speaker cones within one piece of equipment: a woofer for low frequencies; a tweeter for high frequencies; and a midrange speaker for midrange frequencies.

THRESHOLD OF COMPRESSION   The level of signal needed to activate a compressor.

"THROW A PATCH"   Make a connection between an input and output jack on a patch bay by means of a patchcord.

TIMBRE   The relative strength of all the component frequencies in a complex or natural sound; "tone color" or quality. One of the characteristics of sound, by which it is described or compared.

TIME CODE OR SMPTE TIME CODE   SMPTE Time Code is an electronic signal which can be recorded on an audio or video tape and which can be read as running time in hours, minutes, and frames (one thirtieth of a second). It is also commonly used to synchronize two or more audio and/or video tapes. Using time code, two 24 track tape recorders can act as if they were one 48 track machine; both machines will fast-forward, re-wind, stop, and play together in perfect unison following a slight delay during which the code on one machine is compared with the code on the other. The time code is usually recorded on the 24th track of a 24 track recorder, and the 23rd track is often left blank to avoid leakage between the time code and what might otherwise be put on track 23. This means that if two 24 track machines are linked via time code there are usually only 44 tracks available for recording program material.

TIP-RING   A "mono," two-conductor phone connector.

TIP-RING-SLEEVE   A "stereo," three-conductor phone type connector only used for stereo in the case of headphones.

TONE   1. See "pure tone." 2. A musical sound formed by a complex of frequencies; often used with reference to pitch.

TONE ARM   The phonograph part containing the stylus and cartridge.

TONE COLOR   See "timbre."

TONE GENERATOR   See "oscillator."

TRACK   1. (*noun*) The actual part of a tape where a signal is recorded; each track on a tape can contain a separate channel with separate information contained in the signals recorded in that track. (Thus stereo recording necessitates at least two tracks.) 2. (*verb*) Referring to a stylus, to ride in the grooves of phonograph record.

TRACK CONFIGURATION   The number of separate, distinct audio channels that can be recorded on a single tape by a particular tape recorder and their position on the tape itself. Track configurations commonly used are full-track (mono only), half-track and quarter-track (mono or stereo); multi-track tape recorders can record more than two channels at once.

TRACKING FORCE   The pressure exerted downward on the stylus by the tone arm of a phonograph.

TRACKING FORCE GAUGE   A device used to measure for adjustment purposes the tracking force of any phonograph.

TRAILER TAPE   Leader tape used for the tail of a program.

TRANSDUCER   A device that converts one form of energy or signal into an analogous form; loudspeakers, cartridges, microphones and tape heads are all transducers.

TRANSFORMER   An electronic device that transfers energy so that its frequency remains the same, but its impedance or its level is changed; used to match impedances and levels between different devices or circuits.

TRANSIENT RESPONSE   The degree to which a device is capable of reproducing a succession of very brief sounds or signals.

TRANSMITTER   A device that combines audio signals with radio frequency signals, so that the audio can be radiated through the air to radio receivers located elsewhere.

TRANSPORT   The part of a tape machine which moves the tape.

TRANSPORT FUNCTION CONTROLS   The switches on the front panel of a tape machine's electronics which control the movement and speed of the tape.

TREBLE   See "high range."

TUNE   1. To adjust a receiving device so that it will most accurately reproduce the frequency of a desired signal being transmitted. 2. To adjust a machine so that it is working optimally.

TUNER   A common name for a radio receiver.

TURNTABLE   The part of a phonograph upon which the record rests as it revolves.

TWEETER   A speaker cone specially designed to optimally reproduce only high frequencies.

TWO-HEAD TAPE RECORDER   A tape recorder in which the recording and playback elements are located in the same head, such as cheaper portable cassette machines.

TWO-WAY SPEAKER SYSTEM   One in which low frequencies are reproduced by a woofer cone and high frequencies by a tweeter.

TYPE A DOLBY®   The Dolby® noise reduction system used in most professional applications, which reduces noise in four separate and strategic frequency ranges.

TYPE B DOLBY®   The Dolby® noise reduction system found in cassette machines and home FM receivers, which reduces only high frequency noise.

TYPE C DOLBY®   Reduces high frequency noice twice as much as "B".

TYPE SR DOLBY®   Reduces noise at many frequencies approximately twice as much as "A".

UNBALANCED CONNECTION   Any connection between two audio devices where only two wires are used, so that at any instant one wire carries the desired signal and the other wire is the "ground;" an unbalanced line is more susceptible to the induction of unwanted signal (hum from a power line, for example) into an audio circuit.

UNIDIRECTIONAL   A microphone with a cardioid (heart-shaped) pickup pattern, designed to respond well to sounds coming from only one specific on-axis direction; used in most close miking situations because of its rejection of other sound sources which might be nearby.

VOICE-OVER   A voice mixed to the "foreground" over a "background" of music, sound effects, or other voices.

VOLT   A unit of measurement for electrical amplitude.

VOLTAGE   The force that causes electrical current to flow through a conductor.

VOLTAGE POTENTIOMETER   See "potentiometer."

VOLUME   The intensity of a sound or electrical signal.

VOLUME UNIT METER   A meter used for audio work which indicates changes in the average volume of a signal; also called "VU meter."

VU METER   See "volume unit meter."

WATT   A unit of measurement for electrical power.

WINCHESTER   A kind of hard, magnetic disk on which digital signals can be recorded.

WINDSCREEN   A foam or other kind of covering for a microphone that shields it from the effects of wind noise and popping.

WOOFER   A speaker cone specially designed to optimally reproduce only low frequencies.

WOW   Pitch change caused by slight variations in the speed of a tape machine or phonograph turntable.

XLR CONNECTOR   See "cannon connector."

Y-ADAPTER   A cable with one connector at one end but two connectors on the other end.

Z   The symbol for impedance.

ZERO VU   The standard reference point, on a VU meter, against which the relative levels of audio signals are measured.

INDEX